LINDA BEACH

Cryptocurrency Trading Essentials

Concepts Made Simple So You Can Develop a Trading Strategy

KAY LANDON BOOKS

First published by Kay Landon Books 2025

First edition

ISBN: 979-8-2954-7063-9

This book was professionally typeset on Reedsy.
Find out more at reedsy.com

Contents

Introduction

In the heart of New York City, a young professional named Sarah found herself at a crossroads. Despite a stable job and a decent salary, she felt trapped in a cycle of living paycheck to paycheck, unable to build the financial future she dreamed of. That's when a friend introduced her to the world of cryptocurrency trading. At first, Sarah was skeptical—the jargon and complexity seemed overwhelming. But as she began to explore further, she realized that with the right knowledge and strategy, cryptocurrency could be the key to unlocking financial freedom.

Sarah's story is not unique. Countless adults today are searching for ways to break free from traditional investment limitations and take control of their financial destiny. The allure of cryptocurrency trading is undeniable—the potential for significant returns, the excitement of participating in a cutting-edge market, and the freedom to invest on your own terms. However, the path to success in this dynamic landscape is not always clear.

That's where this book comes in. "Cryptocurrency Trading Essentials: Concepts Made Simple So You Can Develop a Trading Strategy" is designed to bridge the gap between curiosity and confidence for adults interested in investing in cryptocurrencies. By breaking down complex concepts into easily digestible insights, this book aims to empower you with the knowledge and tools necessary to navigate the crypto market with ease.

As an author, my passion lies in helping individuals like you unlock the doors to financial opportunity. I have witnessed firsthand the transformative potential of this technology.

I first began learning about Bitcoin in 2017. My friend Jeffrey started talking to me about it because this exciting new investment opportunity had just jumped from $1,000 to $3,000. I started listening to what he had to say. While he was talking, I saw it rise to $5,000. This was exciting. I'd never seen a stock jump this way before. So, I started setting up my accounts. By the time my accounts were verified and active, and in only a few weeks' time from the time I had first heard of Bitcoin, this digital coin was now worth $8,500. I put $1,000 into it, and it immediately multiplied. So I began researching what it actually was and learning what it was about.

The more I read, the more I came to believe that cryptocurrency was not a fad, but was the currency of the future. I started reading and studying the whitepapers of the different digital tokens and learning what their actual uses are in the blockchain technology so that I could make informed decisions about which currencies were good for short-term gains and which had long-term potential. (We'll explore whitepapers in chapter 2.) I continued putting money in a little at a time, and my money was multiplying everyday. So every night I was day trading for altcoins, moving my currency around, and watching it grow. I had read enough to know that the technology was here to stay, but I knew nothing about investing. Within a month or so, Bitcoin was worth $17,000! I was convinced it was a good investment, and I wanted to multiply my savings. My intention was to keep some of my money invested in it for the long run, but my plan was to multiply most of my funds short-term and then pull them back out. At the end of 2017, I dumped my entire savings account into Bitcoin and alt currencies. And then it crashed.

That's when I learned the value of HODLing. *Holding on for Dear Life!* It was a roller coaster ride I will never forget. I learned a lot about investing very fast. If I hadn't studied what the cryptocurrencies actually were, and I hadn't come to believe in the technology as a long-term holding, it would have been hard for me to keep holding onto my digital assets through the fall. But I did know all of that, and I believed with all my heart that in a few years, the huge rolling hill of $17,000 crashing back down to $1,000 was going to be a minuscule ripple on the long-term chart. So I banked on it and held my assets. And I was right.

My goal is to make these concepts accessible to everyone, regardless of their background or experience level.

Throughout this book, we will explore the fundamental building blocks of cryptocurrency trading. From understanding the basics of blockchain technology to mastering investment strategies and risk management techniques, each chapter is crafted to provide you with actionable insights and practical guidance. You'll learn how to choose a reliable exchange, diversify your portfolio, analyze market trends, and secure your digital assets with confidence.

But this book is more than just a collection of information—it's a roadmap to financial empowerment. By delving into the pages that follow, you'll gain the tools and knowledge needed to make informed decisions, avoid common pitfalls, and seize opportunities in the ever-evolving world of cryptocurrency.

Whether you're a complete beginner or have some experience with trading, this book is designed to meet you where you are. Each chapter builds upon the last, allowing you to develop a comprehensive understanding of cryptocurrency trading at your own pace. From the fundamentals of blockchain to advanced trading strategies, you'll find insights and guidance suitable for every stage of your journey.

As you progress through the book, I encourage you to approach each lesson with an open mind and a willingness to learn. The world of cryptocurrency is vast and constantly evolving, but with the right mindset and guidance, you can navigate it with confidence. Take the time to absorb the concepts, apply the strategies, and reflect on your own goals and risk tolerance.

Remember, investing in cryptocurrencies is not a get-rich-quick scheme, but rather a path to long-term financial growth and independence. By arming yourself with knowledge and developing a solid trading strategy, you can take control of your financial future and unlock the potential of this exciting market.

So, whether you're driven by the desire for financial freedom, the thrill of participating in a revolutionary technology, or simply the curiosity to explore a new world of investment opportunities, this book is your companion on the journey ahead. Let's dive in together and discover how cryptocurrency trading can transform your financial landscape.

Are you ready to embark on a path towards financial freedom? Turn the page, and let's get started.

1

Chapter 1: Understanding Cryptocurrency and Blockchain Fundamentals

1.1 What is cryptocurrency?

Cryptocurrency is a type of digital or virtual currency that relies on cryptographic techniques for security. Unlike traditional fiat currencies, cryptocurrencies are decentralized and operate on blockchain technology. This decentralization means that cryptocurrencies are not controlled by any government or central authority, allowing for peer-to-peer transactions across the globe.

Cryptocurrencies are digital, meaning they exist only in electronic form. They do not have a physical counterpart like paper money or coins. Instead, they are stored in digital wallets, which allow users to send and receive cryptocurrency via blockchain networks. I'll explain the blockchain in the next section.

Use of Cryptography for Security

Cryptography is fundamental to cryptocurrency's operation. Each transaction is secured using cryptographic algorithms that ensure privacy, integrity, and security. Cryptographic keys are used to verify the ownership of cryptocurrency and authorize transactions, ensuring that only the rightful owner can spend their funds.

Bitcoin and Its Pioneering Role

Bitcoin (BTC) was the first cryptocurrency, introduced in 2009 by the mysterious figure known as **Satoshi Nakamoto**. Bitcoin introduced the concept of decentralized digital currency, enabling peer-to-peer transactions without the need for a central authority like a bank or payment processor. Bitcoin's creation marked the beginning of a new era in finance, offering a decentralized alternative to traditional banking systems and fostering the development of the blockchain technology that underpins all cryptocurrencies today.

Various Altcoins and Their Unique Features

Since Bitcoin's inception, thousands of alternative cryptocurrencies (altcoins) have emerged, each offering unique features and use cases:

Ethereum and Smart Contracts

Ethereum, (ETH) introduced in 2015 by Vitalik Buterin, is Bitcoin's largest competitor. It's a decentralized platform that enables developers to build and deploy **smart contracts**—self-executing contracts with the terms of the agreement directly written into code. Ethereum's blockchain allows for decentralized applications (dApps) to run, expanding the potential of blockchain beyond currency. We'll explore that a little further down.

Ripple and Cross-Border Payment Solutions

Ripple (XRP) focuses on providing fast and low-cost **cross-border payments**. Its RippleNet network allows financial institutions to send and receive money across borders without relying on traditional payment systems like SWIFT, making international transactions faster and more affordable.

Litecoin and Transaction Speed

Litecoin (LTC) is a peer-to-peer cryptocurrency that was designed to be a faster and more scalable alternative to Bitcoin. Being more scalable means the network is better able to handle large amounts of transactions without compromising performance. Litecoin's block generation time is four times faster than Bitcoin's, allowing for quicker transaction processing and lower fees.

Monero and Privacy-Focused Features

Monero (XMR) is a privacy-focused cryptocurrency that uses advanced cryptographic techniques like **ring signatures** and **stealth addresses** to ensure that transactions are private and untraceable. Monero offers a high level of privacy for users who wish to keep their financial transactions anonymous.

These are just a few of the early cryptocurrencies. Today, thousands of currencies exist to choose from.

The Importance of Cryptocurrency in Modern Finance

Cryptocurrencies are reshaping the global financial system by providing alternatives to traditional banking and investment models. A key component of cryptocurrency finance is the **disintermediation of banks.** By eliminating the need for banks and intermediaries, cryptocurrencies enable direct peer-to-peer transactions, as previously mentioned. This reduces fees and processing times. This disintermediation has the potential to democratize financial services, especially in areas where traditional banking infrastructure is lacking. Cryptocurrencies fill in infrastructure gaps by providing **global financial inclusion**, which means they provide financial services to the **unbanked**—those who don't have access to traditional banking systems, particularly in underdeveloped countries. With just a smartphone and an internet connection, anyone can participate in the global economy, send money across borders, and invest in digital assets. This has been a significant advancement for people in countries where banking resources are less available.

Cryptocurrencies also offer new opportunities for **investment diversification**. As a relatively new asset class, cryptocurrencies provide a hedge against inflation and traditional market risks, making them an attractive option for investors looking to expand their portfolios. This will be explored in detail in chapter 2.

1.2 What is Blockchain? A Simple Breakdown

At its most fundamental level, **blockchain** is a **public ledger system** that records transactions in a decentralized and immutable (unchangeable) manner. Let's break that down. Each transaction or piece of data is stored in a "block," and these blocks are linked together to form a chain. The ledger is shared and distributed across all participants in the network, making it transparent and resistant to tampering or central control.

Blockchain technology has rapidly transformed the way the world approaches data storage, security, and transactions. Originally created as the underlying infrastructure for Bitcoin, blockchain has far-reaching applications beyond cryptocurrencies. Let's explore what blockchain is, its key features, and its transformative potential.

Public Ledger System

A public ledger refers to the fact that anyone participating in the blockchain network can access and view the entire transaction history. For example, in Bitcoin, every transaction made with Bitcoin can be publicly verified by anyone using a blockchain explorer. This openness fosters trust, as anyone can audit the system without needing to rely on a centralized authority. Moreover, it eliminates the need for intermediaries, such as banks, to verify transactions.

Decentralization and Its Advantages

Decentralization is one of the most profound aspects of blockchain technology. In traditional systems, central authorities such as banks or governments control transactions and data flow. In a blockchain, however, power is distributed across a decentralized network of computers, known as nodes. Each node stores a copy of the entire blockchain, and consensus mechanisms are used to validate transactions.

The advantages of decentralization are numerous:

- **No Single Point of Failure**: The absence of a central authority means that there is no single point of failure. The system remains operational even if some nodes go offline.
- **Increased Security**: Decentralization makes blockchain more resistant

to attacks. To alter any part of the blockchain, a malicious actor would need to control over 51% of the network, which is nearly impossible in large, well-established networks.

- **Improved Transparency**: Because all transactions are recorded publicly, it's easy to trace and verify transactions, reducing the possibility of fraud.

Immutable Records

Once a block is added to the blockchain, it becomes **immutable**, meaning it cannot be altered or deleted. This immutability is achieved through the use of **cryptographic hash functions**. A hash function takes an input (such as transaction data) and generates a fixed-length string of characters, the hash. Each block in the blockchain contains the hash of the previous block, ensuring that altering any transaction would require changing every subsequent block in the chain, which is computationally impractical. This immutability ensures that data on the blockchain remains tamper-proof, fostering trust and enabling its use in applications requiring secure record-keeping.

Cryptographic Security

As stated above, blockchain relies heavily on **cryptographic security** to protect the integrity of data. Public and private keys are essential components of blockchain's security mechanism. Public keys serve as addresses that users can share to receive cryptocurrency, while private keys are used to sign transactions and verify ownership of the funds. This system ensures that only the rightful owner of a cryptocurrency can authorize transactions, preventing unauthorized access and theft.

The Benefits of Blockchain

Beyond cryptocurrency, blockchain technology has a range of applications that can revolutionize industries, from supply chain management to financial services. Below are some of the key benefits blockchain offers across various sectors:

Transparency in Supply Chains

One of the most impactful uses of blockchain is in improving **supply chain transparency**. Traditional supply chains are often opaque, with multiple intermediaries that can obscure the flow of goods and information. Blockchain, however, provides an immutable and transparent record of every step in the supply chain process. Each product's journey—from raw material sourcing to delivery—can be tracked in real time, increasing accountability and reducing fraud. This is particularly beneficial in industries like food and pharmaceuticals, where transparency is critical for ensuring safety and quality. Blockchain allows for more efficient recalls, as affected products can be traced back to their origin quickly and accurately.

Enhanced Security in Data Management

Blockchain's cryptographic security makes it an excellent solution for **data management**. By using decentralized storage and encryption, sensitive data can be kept secure from hacking and unauthorized access. This is especially important in industries like healthcare, where patient data needs to be securely stored and shared.

Blockchain can also be used to create secure digital identities, enabling individuals to control access to their personal information. Instead of relying on centralized systems like social media platforms or banks to verify identity, blockchain allows for self-sovereign identities that are more resistant to data breaches.

Streamlining Financial Transactions

As already stated, blockchain has the potential to **streamline financial transactions** by providing faster, cheaper, and more secure alternatives to traditional banking systems. With the ability to conduct **peer-to-peer transactions**, users can send money across borders without relying on intermediaries, significantly reducing fees and processing times.

In addition to international transfers, blockchain can also be used for smart contracts—self-executing contracts where terms are automatically executed once certain conditions are met. This can eliminate the need for middlemen in various industries, from real estate to insurance, and significantly reduce the potential for human error or fraud.

The Structure of a Block

Each block in a blockchain has several key components that work together to ensure the integrity and security of the system.

Block Header

A **block header** contains important metadata about the block. It typically includes a **hash of the block**. This is a unique identifier generated by hashing the block's contents. This hash is used to link the block to the previous one. The **previous block hash** is a reference to the hash of the preceding block in the chain, ensuring that the blocks are linked together in the correct order. The block also includes a **timestamp**, which is the time when the block was created. This provides a chronological order to the blockchain.

Transactions and Data Storage

In addition to the block header, each block contains a list of **transactions**. Each transaction includes the sender's public key, the recipient's public key, the amount of cryptocurrency being transferred, and other relevant details. The block also contains a **Merkle tree**, a cryptographic structure that summarizes all the transactions in the block and allows for efficient verification of their authenticity.

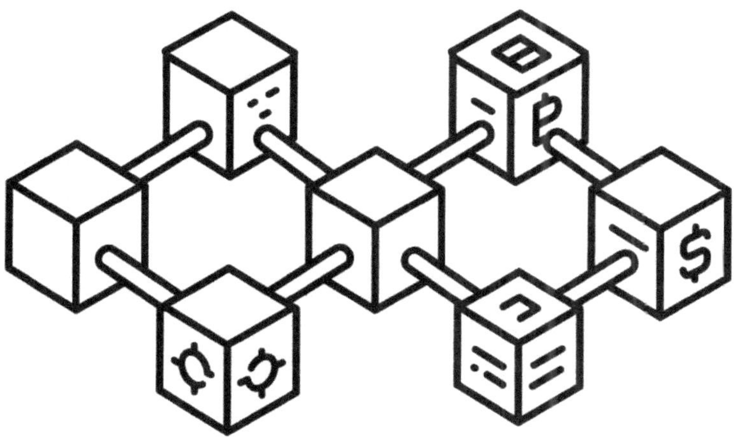

Blockchain Consensus Mechanisms

One of the most important aspects of blockchain is how transactions are validated and added to the blockchain. This process is governed by **consensus mechanisms**, which are protocols that ensure all participants in the network agree on the state of the blockchain.

Who Are the Validators?

Bitcoin validators, commonly referred to as **miners** or **nodes**, play a crucial role in the Bitcoin network by verifying and maintaining its decentralized ledger. Here's a breakdown of their roles and differences:

Miners validate new transactions and package them into blocks. They secure the network by solving complex mathematical problems (proof-of-work) to add a new block to the blockchain. Miners are rewarded with newly minted bitcoins (block rewards) and transaction fees when they successfully mine a block. Mining typically requires specialized hardware known as ASICs (Application-Specific Integrated Circuits).

Nodes validate all transactions and blocks independently by adhering to Bitcoin's consensus rules (e.g., block size, difficulty, etc.). They maintain a complete copy of the blockchain. Unlike minors, nodes do not create new blocks but ensure that all transactions and blocks follow Bitcoin's protocol rules. Full nodes help enforce the network's decentralization by rejecting invalid blocks or transactions, even if miners attempt to include them.

Anyone can run a node. Running a Bitcoin node only requires a computer, internet connection, and sufficient storage space for the blockchain. Conversely, mining is competitive. To succeed as a miner, substantial computational power is typically required due to the high level of competition in Bitcoin mining. Both miners and nodes are essential validators in ensuring the integrity and trustworthiness of the Bitcoin blockchain. Let's take a look at some of the key aspects of both approaches.

Mining

Mining is an integral part of the consensus mechanism for validating transactions on the Bitcoin network. Miners collect unconfirmed transactions from the network, validate them, and bundle them into a candidate block. Miners also contribute to the mechanism through **proof of work (PoW)**.

Proof of Work (PoW) is the consensus mechanism used by Bitcoin and many other blockchains. To add a block to the blockchain, miners must solve a complex mathematical puzzle by finding a hash that meets Bitcoin's difficulty target. In PoW, miners compete to be the first to solve these complex mathematical puzzles that require significant computational resources. The first miner to solve the puzzle gets to add the next block to the blockchain and is rewarded with cryptocurrency. PoW ensures that only valid transactions are added to the blockchain, making it resistant to fraud and tampering. While PoW is effective, it is also energy-intensive and can be slow, leading to concerns about its scalability.

Consensus is reached through mining. The first miner to solve the puzzle broadcasts their solution (the block) to the network. Other nodes validate the block's transactions and the PoW before adding it to their copy of the blockchain. A system of **chain agreement** is also built into the mechanism. Bitcoin's consensus rules dictate that the longest valid chain (the one with the most accumulated work) is considered the "true" blockchain. This prevents conflicting versions of the ledger.

Mining secures the network first, by contributing to the **prevention of double spending**. Mining ensures that transactions are ordered chronologically and prevents double spending by requiring substantial computational effort to alter previous blocks. Mining also plays a part in the **attack resistance** of the blockchain. Changing a block would require re-mining that block and all subsequent blocks, which would demand immense computational resources. And mining contributes to the **decentralization** of the blockchain because miners operate independently across the globe, making it difficult for a single entity to control the blockchain.

There are a number of incentives for minors to contribute to the blockchain. The primary incentive is the earning of **block rewards**. Miners receive newly minted bitcoins (currently 6.25 BTC per block, as of 2025) for successfully mining a block. The second main incentive for mining is the earning of **transaction fees**. Miners also collect fees from the transactions included in the block, providing this additional incentive.

Mining is essential to a cryptocurrency's consensus because it enforces agreement across all participants without relying on an authority. The PoW mechanism ensures fairness by requiring energy expenditure for participation. Consensus is achieved because only valid blocks (those meeting the network's rules) are accepted by the nodes.

To wrap up this part, mining is a fundamental part of Bitcoin's and other cryptocurrencies' consensus mechanisms. It validates transactions, secures the network, and ensures that all participants agree on the state of the blockchain through Proof of Work. Without mining, the decentralized trust model that Bitcoin relies on would not function.

An alternative to proof of work mechanism that some of the other cryptocurrencies use is Proof of Stake (PoS). Proof of stake is used as the alternative consensus mechanism by blockchains such as Bitcoin's most competitive rival, Ethereum (after its transition to Ethereum 2.0). In PoS, validators (also known as "stakers") lock up a certain amount of cryptocurrency as collateral. The network selects a validator to create a new block based on the amount of cryptocurrency they have staked and other factors. Validators are rewarded with transaction fees and block rewards for their work. PoS is considered more energy-efficient than PoW and is gaining popularity as a more sustainable way to secure blockchain networks. Two other popular cryptocurrencies that allow holders to stake their assets are Cardano (ADA) and Polkadot (DOT).

In addition to the PoW and PoS mechanisms, transactions in the blockchain are also validated by running nodes.

Running Nodes

Running a Bitcoin node provides indirect incentives, but it does not offer direct financial rewards like mining.

There are a number of key incentives for running a cryptocurrency node:

- **Enhanced Security and Privacy:** By running a full node, users validate all transactions and blocks independently. This ensures they are interacting with a completely trustworthy and tamper-proof version of the Bitcoin network. Running a node also eliminates reliance on third parties. Users do not need to trust external nodes or centralized services to verify their transactions. Further running a node provides users with enhanced privacy. A node allows users to broadcast their transactions directly to the network without exposing them to external servers, preserving anonymity.
- **Contribution to Decentralization:** Running a node strengthens the Bitcoin network by increasing its decentralization. A higher number of nodes makes it harder for bad actors to attack or manipulate the network.
- **Support for the Bitcoin Ecosystem:** Nodes help relay transactions and blocks to other nodes, ensuring the network remains fast, efficient, and reliable. By maintaining and propagating the blockchain, nodes contribute to the Bitcoin ecosystem, making it accessible to other

participants.

- **Control and Empowerment:** Node operators can enforce their own custom policy rules, such as rejecting transactions that don't meet certain criteria (e.g., minimum fees).
- **Direct Access to Data:** Users gain complete access to the blockchain's data for analysis or development purposes without relying on third-party services.
- **Minimal Expenses:** Unlike mining, running a Bitcoin node is relatively inexpensive. It primarily requires:
- *A computer.*
- *Sufficient storage (about 500 GB or more as of 2025).*
- *A stable internet connection.*

Who Typically Runs a Node?

Nodes are typically run by cryptocurrency enthusiasts, businesses, and developers. Enthusiast include people who value the currency's decentralization and want to support the network. Businesses such as exchanges, payment processors, and wallet providers run nodes to ensure reliable transaction verification and a high level of trust for their services. And developers working on cryptocurrency-related applications use nodes for testing and building. The incentive to run a cryptocurrency node is not financial but rather rooted in security, control, privacy, and supporting the currency's decentralized ethos. It's a way to actively participate in and uphold the integrity of the network.

1.3 How Cryptocurrency Transactions Work

The Process of a Cryptocurrency Transaction

A typical cryptocurrency transaction involves several steps, including initiating the transaction, broadcasting it to the network, and validating it.

1. **Initiating a Transaction with a Digital Wallet**: The process begins when the user creates a transaction using their digital wallet. This wallet stores their public and private keys and enables them to send cryptocurrency to other users.
2. **Broadcast to the Network for Validation:** Once the transaction is initiated, it is broadcast to the network, where —
3. — nodes and miners **validate the transaction**.

1.4 Important Cryptocurrency Platforms and Services

Several platforms provide critical services and resources to crypto enthusiasts and investors. When entering the world of cryptocurrencies, one of the first and most important decisions is selecting the right cryptocurrency exchange. The **exchange** is the platform that allows users to buy, sell, and trade digital assets. There are several types of exchanges, each with distinct features and functionalities. Understanding the differences between these exchanges will help you make an informed choice.

Types of Cryptocurrency Exchanges

Centralized Exchanges (CEX) are the most commonly used platforms for trading cryptocurrencies. Examples include Binance, Coinbase, Kraken, and Bitfinex. Centralized exchanges function as intermediaries between buyers and sellers, acting as custodians for users' funds. These exchanges are typically more user-friendly and offer a wide range of services, including advanced trading tools, fiat-to-crypto pairs, and customer support. The main advantage of using a centralized exchange is that it provides an easy and familiar interface for new users. However, the key drawback is that users must trust the exchange to manage their funds. Centralized exchanges are also more vulnerable to hacking, as they store large amounts of cryptocurrency in hot wallets. We'll explore the pros and cons of different types of wallets in chapter 3.

Decentralized Exchanges (DEX), such as Uniswap and SushiSwap, operate without a central authority. Instead of relying on a third party to facilitate transactions, decentralized exchanges use smart contracts to enable peer-to-peer trading. This means users maintain full control of their funds throughout the transaction process. DEXs are generally considered more secure because there is no central point of failure, and users can trade directly from their wallets. However, they tend to have lower liquidity and fewer trading pairs compared to centralized exchanges. Additionally, DEXs often provide a steeper learning curve for beginners due to the decentralized nature of the platform.

Hybrid Exchanges combine the features of both centralized and decentralized exchanges. Examples include Gemini, Qurrex, Kucoin, and Crypto.com. These exchanges aim to offer the ease of use and liquidity of centralized exchanges while providing the security and decentralization benefits of DEXs. They usually function by allowing users to trade in a decentralized manner while offering additional services like margin trading, staking, or a central order book for better liquidity. The goal of hybrid exchanges is to provide a balance between speed, security, and user autonomy, but these platforms are still relatively new compared to the more established options in the market.

Factors to Consider When Selecting an Exchange

When selecting an exchange, it is important to evaluate several key factors to ensure you are choosing a platform that fits your needs:

Security Measures and Insurance Policies are essential when evaluating an exchange. Since cryptocurrency transactions are irreversible, choosing an exchange with robust security protocols is crucial to protect your assets. Look for exchanges that employ industry-standard security features such as two-factor authentication (2FA), encryption, and cold storage of funds. Additionally, some exchanges offer insurance policies to protect user funds in case of a hack or breach, although the extent of this coverage varies by platform.

User Interface and Ease of Use is another important consideration, particularly for beginners. The exchange's interface should be intuitive and easy to navigate, allowing you to trade quickly and efficiently. A clean and well-designed platform can make the trading experience more enjoyable and reduce the chances of mistakes. Many exchanges also offer mobile apps for on-the-go trading, so it's worth considering whether the exchange provides a smooth mobile experience.

Trading Fees and Limits are significant factors that can influence your overall trading experience. Every exchange charges fees, whether they are flat rates or percentage-based, and these fees can vary widely depending on the platform. Consider both trading fees and withdrawal fees, as these can add up over time. Some exchanges also impose minimum or maximum deposit and withdrawal limits, so ensure the platform supports the amount of trading activity you intend to conduct.

Supported Currencies and Trading Pairs are another important factor when choosing an exchange. Some exchanges offer a wide variety of cryptocurrencies, including altcoins, while others may focus primarily on

Bitcoin and Ethereum. Be sure that the exchange supports the coins and tokens you want to trade, and check the available trading pairs to ensure the exchange meets your trading needs.

The Importance of Regulatory Compliance — When selecting an exchange, **regulatory compliance** is critical to ensure that the platform operates legally and ethically. The cryptocurrency industry is still developing, and regulatory standards can vary significantly by jurisdiction. However, exchanges that comply with **Know Your Customer (KYC)** and **Anti-Money Laundering (AML)** regulations are typically more reliable. These procedures help verify the identity of users and prevent illicit activities like money laundering or fraud. Many reputable exchanges require users to submit identification documents as part of the account creation process to comply with these standards.

Additionally, exchanges that are **registered with financial authorities** or have obtained licenses from regulatory bodies in their respective jurisdictions are generally considered safer. For instance, exchanges operating in the United States must comply with the regulations set forth by the **Securities and Exchange Commission (SEC)** or the **Commodity Futures Trading Commission (CFTC)**. By choosing an exchange that adheres to these legal standards, you are more likely to experience a safe and regulated trading environment. Exchanges that are in compliance typically include a disclosure statement on their website to indicate their regulatory status. Generally speaking, exchange adherence to KYC and AML is a good indicator of compliance.

Tracking Apps

Managing a diversified cryptocurrency portfolio requires tools and strategies for tracking assets and monitoring performance. **Portfolio tracking apps** like Blockfolio and Delta are popular platforms that allow investors to view their holdings in real-time and track price movements. These apps help users stay informed and make adjustments to their portfolio when necessary.

For example, CoinMarketCap is a widely used platform for tracking cryptocurrency prices, market capitalization, trading volume, and other relevant data. It offers a comprehensive overview of the crypto market, helping users stay informed about market trends and performance.

Blockchain Explorers, such as Etherscan and Blockchain.com, allow users to track transactions and view data on various blockchains. These explorers provide transparency and allow users to verify transactions, ensuring that they are recorded correctly on the blockchain. Cointracker is a portfolio tracking app that integrates with exchanges to help users keep up with important tax information. We'll explore the tax requirements in trading cryptocurrencies in detail in chapter 6.

* * *

In conclusion, this chapter provided an in-depth look at blockchain and cryptocurrency, breaking down the core concepts and mechanisms that drive this transformative technology. From its decentralized nature to its potential in various industries, blockchain is reshaping the way we view transactions, security, and financial systems. Cryptocurrency, fueled by this innovative technology, offers a glimpse into the future of finance, where decentralization, transparency, and efficiency are the norms. In the next several chapters, we'll take a look at ways to maximize investments using these technologies.

2

Chapter 2: Investment Strategies and Portfolio Diversification

2.1 The Basics of Cryptocurrency Investment

Cryptocurrency investment has become a prominent part of the global financial landscape. As digital currencies like Bitcoin and Ethereum have grown in popularity, many investors have sought to capitalize on the new opportunities offered by this innovative asset class. However, cryptocurrency investment differs significantly from traditional investments, and understanding its unique characteristics is essential for success. In this chapter, we will explore the fundamental principles of cryptocurrency investing, the importance of research and due diligence, common investment mistakes, and the value of starting small.

Cryptocurrency Investment Principles

At the core of cryptocurrency investment lies a few fundamental principles that every investor must understand to navigate the market effectively. One of the most important metrics in cryptocurrency investment is **market**

capitalization. Market capitalization is the total value of a cryptocurrency, calculated by multiplying the price of a single coin or token by its total supply. This metric helps investors gauge the relative size and potential of a cryptocurrency. A higher market cap often indicates a more established and widely recognized asset, while smaller cap coins may present higher risks but also greater potential rewards.

Liquidity is another insightful aspect of cryptocurrency markets. Liquidity refers to how easily an asset can be bought or sold without significantly affecting its price. A highly liquid market allows investors to enter or exit positions with ease, minimizing the risk of slippage. Cryptocurrency markets are known for their volatility, and liquidity can vary significantly depending on the coin, exchange, and trading volume. Coins with low liquidity can experience wild price fluctuations, making it essential for investors to understand the liquidity levels of assets they wish to trade.

Before making any investment in cryptocurrency, **research** and **due diligence** are paramount. In contrast to traditional stocks or bonds, cryptocurrencies are often unregulated and can be highly speculative. **Speculative investments** are those in which the value is based on speculated price increases that may or may not occur, as opposed to being based on the utility of the asset. As a result, investors must be proactive in gathering information to evaluate the risks and potential rewards of each investment. We'll explore ways to do this further in this chapter when we get to the section on Fundamental Analysis.

The Importance of Starting Small

Cryptocurrency investing can be daunting, especially for beginners. One of the best approaches to mitigate risk is to start small. By **testing the waters** with modest investments, new investors can learn the ins and outs of the market without exposing themselves to significant losses.

Many exchanges also offer **demo accounts** that allow users to practice trading with virtual funds. These accounts are invaluable tools for building familiarity with the trading platform and understanding market dynamics. By starting small and gradually increasing exposure, investors can gain experience and build confidence before committing larger sums of money.

2.2 Crafting a Diversified Crypto Portfolio

A critical aspect of successful investing in cryptocurrencies is **portfolio diversification**. Diversifying your portfolio helps to mitigate risk and increase the likelihood of returns by spreading investments across different assets. In the volatile world of cryptocurrencies, diversification can act as a hedge against the potential for large losses in any one coin or token.

Diversifying, or spreading investments across different assets, reduces risk. In traditional investing, diversification involves investing in a mix of asset classes like stocks, bonds, and real estate. In cryptocurrency, diversification takes on a different form. By holding a variety of cryptocurrencies, investors can reduce their exposure to any single asset, minimizing the overall risk of the portfolio.

Diversification allows investors to be exposed to **different market sectors** within the crypto space. For example, Bitcoin and Ethereum are the two largest and most well-established cryptocurrencies, while newer altcoins may be riskier but offer potential for higher returns, as they give later investors the opportunity to get in as early adopters as these new currencies are released into the market. Some investors have seen great returns on alt coins that were released for fractions of a penny, such as DOGE and Shiba Inu. However, others have invested in alternative cryptocurrencies that sold for only fractions of penny, only to see some of these unestablished coins dissolve within a few months. A diversified portfolio can balance these assets, offering stability while maintaining growth potential.

Strategies for Effective Diversification

Effective diversification involves careful consideration of which assets to include in your portfolio. One strategy is to allocate investments across different **types of cryptocurrencies**. For example, large-cap cryptocurrencies like Bitcoin and Ethereum can form the foundation of your portfolio, offering stability and long-term growth potential. Smaller altcoins can be added for higher risk, higher potential reward opportunities.

Another useful strategy is incorporating **stablecoins** like USDT (Tether) or USDC (USD Coin) into your portfolio. Stablecoins, which are digital currencies pegged to stable assets like the US dollar, offer a safer entry point for new investors. Being pegged to fiat currencies like the US dollar, these cryptocurrencies' prices remain relatively stable compared to the volatility of other cryptocurrencies. By investing in stablecoins, individuals can gain exposure to the cryptocurrency market without the fear of wild price swings. Holding these currencies can help investors reduce portfolio volatility and maintain liquidity during market downturns.

Within the cryptocurrency market, there are different **asset classes** to consider when diversifying a portfolio. **Utility tokens** are used within a particular blockchain ecosystem and provide access to services or products within that ecosystem. An example is the token **Gas**, which is used by the Ethereum network to pay transaction fees. **Security tokens**, on the other hand, represent ownership in an underlying asset, such as equity or debt, and may be subject to securities regulations.

Non-fungible tokens (**NFTs**) represent unique assets, typically in the form of digital art or collectibles, that are stored on a blockchain. While they have become increasingly popular, NFTs are highly speculative and are generally considered a more niche and volatile part of the cryptocurrency market. Including NFTs in your portfolio can provide exposure to this growing sector but should be approached with caution.

2.3 Understanding Market Volatility and Its Impact

Market volatility in the context of cryptocurrency refers to the extent to which the price of a cryptocurrency fluctuates over a given period. Unlike traditional markets, cryptocurrencies are notorious for their sharp and erratic price movements. While traditional markets such as stocks, bonds, and commodities experience price fluctuations, they tend to be more stable over time. Cryptocurrencies, on the other hand, can witness dramatic price swings in a matter of hours or even minutes. This volatility is often amplified by the speculative nature of crypto markets and their relatively small market size compared to more established asset classes. In this section, we will explore the nature of cryptocurrency market volatility, its causes, and how it impacts investment strategies.

The Nature of Market Volatility

In financial markets, volatility is typically measured by the **volatility index (VIX)**, which gauges market risk based on asset price fluctuations. However, in the cryptocurrency space, a volatility index specific to digital assets is also used. The **Crypto Volatility Index (CVI)** measures the expected price volatility of Bitcoin, Ethereum, and other cryptocurrencies over a given time period. A higher CVI indicates greater market uncertainty, suggesting that cryptocurrencies are prone to larger price swings. The CVI has often been much higher than traditional market volatility indexes, reflecting the speculative and unregulated nature of the crypto market. Cvi.finance is one platform used to track this indicator.

The **historical trends** in cryptocurrency price fluctuations further highlight the inherent volatility. Bitcoin, for example, has witnessed multiple **boom and bust cycles** since its inception in 2009. At various points, its price surged to new heights, only to experience a sharp drop, followed by gradual recovery. In 2017, Bitcoin's price reached an all-time high of nearly $20,000, only to crash back down below $4,000 by 2018. Such drastic price swings can be attributed to several factors, including market sentiment, speculative trading, and external influences like regulatory news or technological developments. For new and seasoned investors alike, understanding these patterns is essential when navigating the crypto space.

Causes of Volatility in the Crypto Market

There are several key factors that contribute to the high volatility seen in cryptocurrency markets. One of the most significant is **market sentiment**. Cryptocurrency prices are highly sensitive to news, events, and public opinion. Positive news, such as large institutional investments in a particular coin or favorable regulatory announcements, can lead to rapid price increases. Conversely, negative news, such as regulatory crackdowns or security breaches, can cause a steep decline in prices. For instance, in 2021, the Chinese government's repeated actions against cryptocurrency mining and trading led to a significant drop in prices across the board. In the absence of strong, consistent fundamentals, the market often moves based on sentiment rather than tangible asset value.

Another contributing factor, mentioned previously, is **liquidity**, the ease with which an asset can be bought or sold without affecting its price. Cryptocurrencies, especially smaller altcoins, can suffer from **low liquidity**, meaning that even small trades can have a significant impact on their prices. When there is a lack of market depth — that is, when there are not enough buy or sell orders at different price levels — the market becomes more susceptible to large price swings. Major cryptocurrencies like Bitcoin and Ethereum have high liquidity, but smaller altcoins may be subject to significant volatility when trading volume is low.

The Impact of Volatility on Investment Strategies

Volatility plays a deep role in shaping **investment strategies** in the crypto market. In particular, investors need to carefully consider whether they are adopting **short-term** or **long-term strategies**. Short-term investors, such as traders who focus on making profits through day trading or swing trading, thrive on volatility, using price swings to their advantage. They seek to capitalize on rapid market changes by buying at lower prices and selling when prices rise. However, this approach requires constant monitoring of the market and a keen understanding of technical analysis.

In contrast, long-term investors, often referred to as "HODLers" in the crypto community, focus on holding their assets over an extended period. These investors are less concerned with short-term price fluctuations and instead focus on the long-term potential of the cryptocurrency. For example, Bitcoin's historical performance has shown strong long-term growth despite its price volatility. By focusing on the underlying value of the asset and its future use cases, long-term investors are more likely to withstand market corrections without making impulsive decisions.

2.4 Balancing Risk and Reward in Crypto Investments

Investing in cryptocurrencies presents both opportunities and risks. The **risk-reward ratio** is a key concept that every cryptocurrency investor should understand. The ratio compares the potential for profit (reward) with the potential for loss (risk) and helps investors make informed decisions based on their investment goals.

Risk management is essential when investing in high-risk assets like cryptocurrencies. One of the first steps in managing risk is to assess your **risk tolerance**. Risk tolerance is the degree to which an investor is comfortable with the possibility of losing money in exchange for the chance of higher returns. A high-risk tolerance may suit aggressive investors, while more conservative investors may prefer to focus on safer assets like Bitcoin or stablecoins.

When evaluating potential investments, it is necessary to assess the risk-reward ratio of each potential asset. Again, high-risk, high-reward opportunities often come with the possibility of significant gains but also carry a higher chance of substantial losses. On the other hand, low-risk, low-reward assets may offer more stability but less potential for rapid growth. By carefully weighing these factors, investors can determine whether an investment aligns with their goals and risk tolerance.

2.5 Risk Management Techniques for Crypto Trading

As stated above, navigating volatile markets requires a strategic approach to managing risk. We talked about diversification to help reduce the impact of price fluctuations in any one coin, offering more stable returns over time. For example, instead of investing all funds into a single cryptocurrency like Bitcoin, an investor might diversify by also holding Ethereum, Litecoin, and stablecoins. In addition to diversification, several other strategies can be employed to mitigate risks in cryptocurrency investments.

One popular risk management strategy is **dollar-cost averaging (DCA)**, which involves investing a fixed amount of money at regular intervals, regardless of the price. This approach helps mitigate the impact of short-term volatility by averaging out the cost of entry over time. DCA is especially useful for investors who are not able to time the market but want to benefit from long-term price appreciation.

Another strategy is **hedging** with stablecoins. During periods of extreme volatility, traders may move a portion of their portfolio into stablecoins like Tether (USDT) or USD Coin (USDC). These assets are pegged to the US dollar and maintain their value, offering a safe haven during market downturns. By holding stablecoins, investors can protect their portfolio from the worst effects of price drops while maintaining the ability to re-enter the market when conditions stabilize.

Risk-reward ratio is a strategy used to assess risk and can be used to help inform decisions. The risk-reward ratio is a measure of how much risk an investor is willing to take in exchange for potential rewards. For example, if an investor risks $100 on a trade with the potential for a $300 return, the risk-reward ratio would be 1:3. Traders typically aim for a favorable risk-reward ratio, ensuring that the potential rewards justify the risks. It's important to know how much you are able to risk, so that your risk-reward ratio fits your budget.

Stop-loss orders are another risk management tool that can help limit losses. A stop-loss order is a type of order placed with a broker to buy or sell an asset when it reaches a particular price. This predetermined price level at which an asset will automatically be sold helps investors limit losses. For example, if an investor purchases Bitcoin at $50,000 and sets a stop-loss order at $48,000, the trade will be automatically closed if the price drops to $48,000. This helps limit potential losses in case the market moves against the investor's position. By setting a stop-loss, investors can automate the process of selling an asset if its price falls below a certain threshold, reducing potential losses.

Take-profit orders are the opposite of stop-loss orders. They are designed to automatically sell an asset when it reaches a certain profit level. For instance, if an investor buys Bitcoin at $50,000 and sets a take-profit order at $60,000, the asset will be sold when the price reaches $60,000, securing the profit. Setting optimal stop-loss and take-profit levels requires a thorough understanding of market conditions, as well as the investor's risk tolerance and investment goals.

When setting stop-loss and take-profit levels, traders should aim for risk-reward ratios that offer higher potential rewards than the risks they are taking. Volatility requires investors to **adjust their strategies** based on the current market conditions. During periods of high volatility, traders may tighten their stop-loss orders to prevent large losses, while also setting higher take-profit targets to capture gains during price surges. Conversely, during periods of low volatility, traders may adjust their risk tolerance by setting wider stop-loss orders and aiming for smaller, more consistent returns.

Hedging is a more complex strategy, involving the use of **derivatives** like **futures** and **options** to protect against adverse price movements. Since cryptocurrency prices can be highly unpredictable, hedging futures and options enables traders to offset the risk of adverse price movements by taking opposing positions in the market. This strategy acts as a financial safeguard, protecting investments from sudden downturns. For instance, a trader holding Bitcoin can short Bitcoin futures to profit if the price falls, balancing potential losses from the asset's depreciation. Similarly, options allow traders to secure the right, but not the obligation, to buy or sell cryptocurrencies at a predetermined price, providing flexibility in risk management. Hedging is not about eliminating risk entirely but rather about minimizing potential losses while preserving opportunities for profit. By employing well-planned hedging strategies, traders can better navigate the unpredictable cryptocurrency market and protect their investments, offsetting potential losses in their crypto holdings with gains in derivative contracts.

The Importance of Portfolio Rebalancing

Regular **portfolio rebalancing** is another essential risk management technique. Over time, the value of assets within a portfolio may change, and certain assets may become overrepresented or underrepresented. For example, if the value of Bitcoin skyrockets while other altcoins stagnate, an investor's portfolio may become heavily weighted toward Bitcoin. Rebalancing involves periodically adjusting the portfolio to maintain the desired asset allocation. This can be done manually or automatically through tools offered by platforms like CoinTracker and Blockfolio. Sometimes I check my portfolio to see if the altcoins I invested in several years ago are still relevant today. If they don't show significant growth over a several year period and they seem to have disappeared from the news, then it might be wise to trade them for a more established currency that has proven more valuable over time.

Using apps to track the market of various cryptocurrencies, both those held in your portfolio and those that might be of interest for you to accrue, helps investors make decisions that are critical for rebalancing. Over time, the value of assets within a portfolio may change, and certain coins may outperform others. Periodically rebalancing your portfolio by trading certain currencies and adding others ensures that your allocations remain aligned with your investment goals. Many platforms also offer automated rebalancing features, which adjust the portfolio based on predefined rules.

Rebalancing helps to maintain a portfolio's risk profile and ensures that investors are not overly exposed to any one asset. While there is no set frequency for rebalancing, it is important to review portfolios regularly to make adjustments based on changes in market conditions, personal risk tolerance, and investment goals.

2.6 Integrating Cryptocurrencies into Traditional Portfolios

As cryptocurrencies gain mainstream acceptance, investors are increasingly looking to integrate them into traditional portfolios. This section explores the benefits of adding crypto to traditional investments, how to balance both asset classes, and regulatory considerations for mixed portfolios.

Benefits of Adding Crypto to Traditional Portfolios

Cryptocurrencies offer several benefits when added to traditional portfolios. First, they provide **potential for higher returns** compared to traditional asset classes like stocks and bonds. Cryptocurrencies have outperformed many other assets over the past decade, attracting investors seeking higher growth. Further, the cryptocurrency market is still relatively new compared to the stock market. As everyone knows, early investors of Apple and Google stock during tech boom are invaluable today, but the window of opportunity for getting those stocks early has closed. Cryptocurrencies still offer some potential for getting in as early investor compared to tech stocks.

Adding crypto also provides **diversification** beyond traditional assets. By holding both traditional and digital assets, investors can protect themselves from market downturns that affect only one asset class. Cryptocurrencies tend to have a low correlation with traditional assets, meaning they may perform well when stocks and bonds are struggling. In a worst-case event of a collapse of traditional currencies, cryptocurrencies may well thrive as a result, much like we see with gold and precious metals.

Balancing Traditional and Crypto Assets

Balancing traditional and crypto assets requires careful thought and strategy. One common approach is to allocate a **percentage of the portfolio** to cryptocurrencies based on the investor's risk tolerance and financial goals. A more conservative investor may allocate just 5-10% to crypto, while a more aggressive investor might increase that allocation.

Regulatory Considerations

As cryptocurrencies become more integrated into traditional portfolios, understanding the **regulatory landscape** is critical. Many countries have different tax regulations regarding cryptocurrency investments, and compliance is essential to avoid legal issues. Investors should also be aware of **capital gains taxes** and other tax implications when selling or trading cryptocurrencies. We'll look at tax implications more closely later in chapter 6.

2.7 Introduction to Technical Analysis in Crypto

Technical analysis (TA) is a method of evaluating financial markets by studying historical price data, volume, and other market-related indicators to forecast future price movements. In the cryptocurrency market, where price fluctuations can be excitingly volatile, technical analysis is essential for traders seeking to make informed decisions based on patterns, trends, and historical data. Through a combination of indicators, chart patterns, and trends, technical analysis offers valuable insights that can guide short-term trading decisions.

Historical Price Data as a Predictive Tool

The foundation of technical analysis rests on the principle that **past market behavior can offer clues about future price movements**. By studying the **historical price data** of a cryptocurrency, traders can identify recurring patterns and trends. In this part, we'll take a look at specific ways to identify patterns.

Price data can also offer insights into market sentiment. An uptrend might indicate optimism among traders, while a downtrend might suggest pessimism. While no prediction is guaranteed, historical price data can provide a roadmap to navigate the volatile cryptocurrency landscape, offering traders insight into potential entry and exit points.

Importance of Chart Patterns and Trends

In technical analysis, **chart patterns** and **market trends** are essential tools for technical analysts, helping investors visualize past price movements. This gives them a crucial role in predicting future movements. Charts are the visual representation of historical price data and provide traders with insights into how a cryptocurrency has behaved in the past. For example, **support** and **resistance** are derived from historical data, helping traders anticipate price movements when a cryptocurrency approaches certain price levels. **Support** is the price at which enough buyers enter the market to keep the price from declining any further during the current run. As buyers enter the market, the price begins to rise again. **Resistance** is the price at which enough sellers enter the market to prevent the price from further rising until the next run.

A **bullish trend** indicates that prices are likely to continue rising, while a **bearish trend** suggests that prices are likely to keep declining. Recognizing and interpreting these patterns is essential for anyone engaged in technical analysis, as it can help traders make informed trading decision by identifying opportunities and managing risk.

Types of Crypto Charts

There are several types of **crypto charts** used in technical analysis:

Line Charts are the simplest form of price visualization. They connect closing prices over a set period, offering a clear overview of price movement.

Candlestick Charts are more complex and provide detailed insights into price movements. Each candlestick represents a specific time period and displays the open, high, low, and close prices. These charts are favored for their ability to show both trend direction and volatility.

Bar Charts are similar to candlestick charts but offer less detail. They are primarily used to compare historical data and analyze price trends over time.

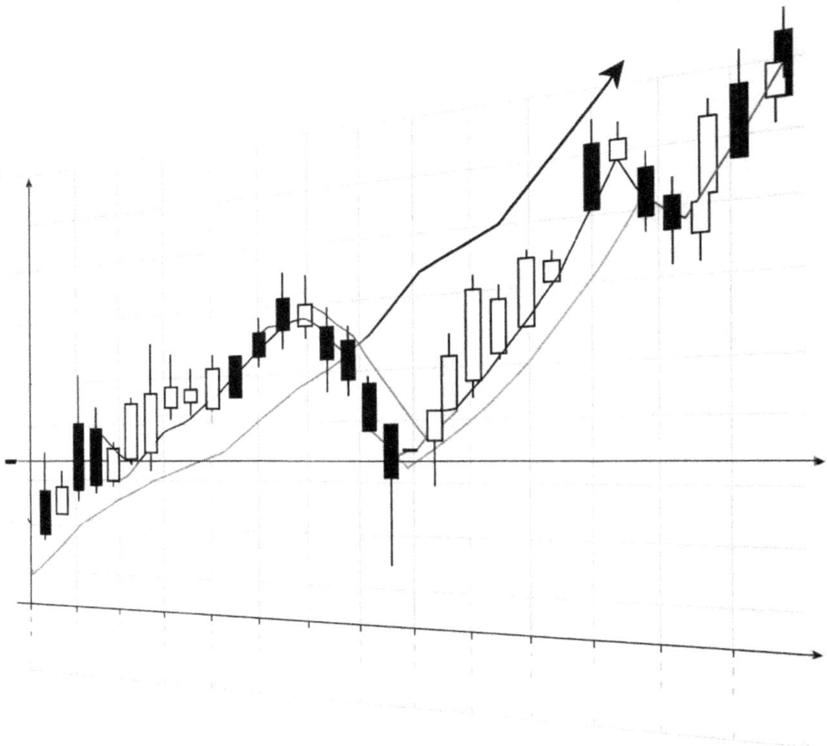

Reading and Interpreting Candlestick Patterns

Candlestick patterns are one of the most widely used tools in technical analysis. Candlesticks that are moving in an upwards direction are green, while downward moving candlesticks are red. Certain patterns, such as the **Hammer**, **Engulfing**, and **Doji**, can indicate potential market reversals or continuation of trends:

Bullish Patterns: The **Hammer** pattern occurs at the bottom of a downtrend, signaling a potential price reversal. In this pattern, the wick of the candle shoots downward and the opening and close for the day are close to each other. An **Engulfing** pattern, where a small candle is followed by a larger one in the opposite direction, can also signal a reversal to the upside. The smaller candle stick gets engulfed by the opposite moving trend.

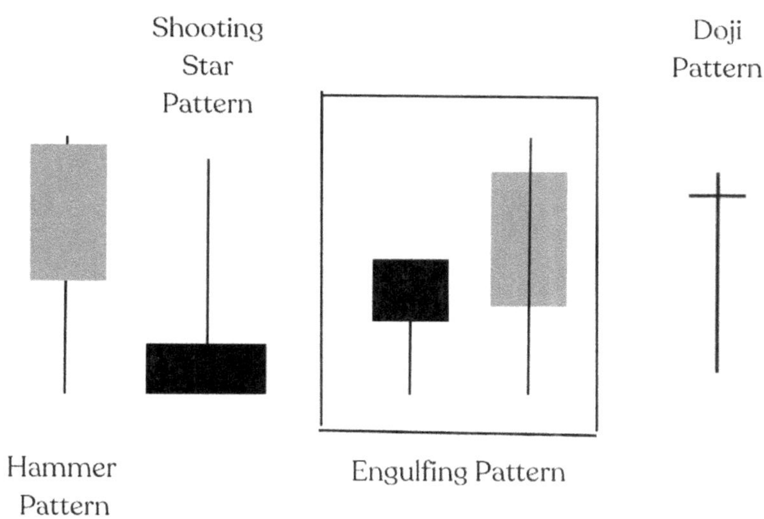

Bearish Patterns: The **Shooting Star** pattern is a bearish reversal pattern that often appears at the top of an uptrend. The opposite of the hammer, it entails the shooting upward of the wick of the candle, only to fall back down and close near the opening price for the same day. The **Doji** pattern, which indicates indecision, can also signal potential reversals depending on its location in the trend. The doji candlestick is short and indicates that the price for the currency opened and closed in similar places with little movement in between.

Trend continuation patterns, such as **flags** and **pennants**, indicate that a trend is likely to continue. Flags and pennants are almost the same. The difference is that flag patterns have parallel convergence lines, while pennant patterns have narrowing pennant lines. In contrast, **reversal patterns** like the **Head and Shoulders** pattern suggest that a trend may be about to reverse.

Application of Chart Patterns in Trading

Trend analysis is the cornerstone of chart analysis. Identifying **ascending** and **descending trends** helps traders make decisions about whether to enter or exit a position. These trend patterns can signal whether an asset is likely to rise, fall, or consolidate. **Chart patterns** like **Head and Shoulders** and **Triangles** are valuable tools for forecasting price movements. A **Head and Shoulders** pattern occurs when a higher peak is accompanied by two "shoulder" peaks, or lower peaks on each side. This typically signals a trend reversal, usually towards a downward shift. A **double top pattern** is an M-shaped pattern in which two significant peaks are side by side. This too is considered a trend reversal pattern that is seen at the end of a rising trend right before the market for the asset begins to fall. Conversely, the **double**

bottom pattern, which is shaped like a W, is considered to indicate the end of a downward trend, reversing towards an upward trend.

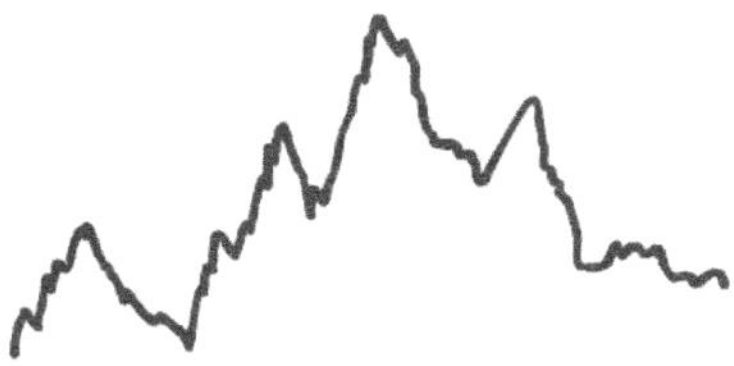

Head and Shoulders Pattern

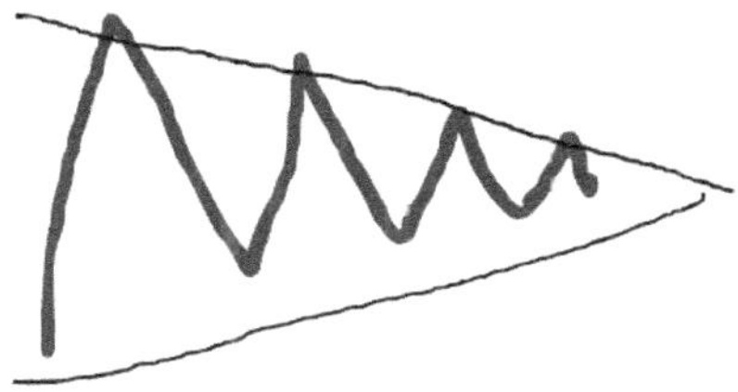

Triangle Pattern

Double Top Pattern

Triangles and **pennants** are chart patterns that indicate that the price is consolidating before a breakout. A triangle pattern occurs when the range of highs and lows narrows, creating a wide left side tightening into a narrow right side. Ascending triangles indicate that the market for the asset is rising, whereas descending triangles indicate a declining market price. A pennant is a triangle trend with an outlying spike on one end.

* * *

Bollinger Bands

Bollinger bands are a popular technical analysis tool used in financial markets to measure market volatility and identify potential trading opportunities. They consist of three lines plotted on a price chart:

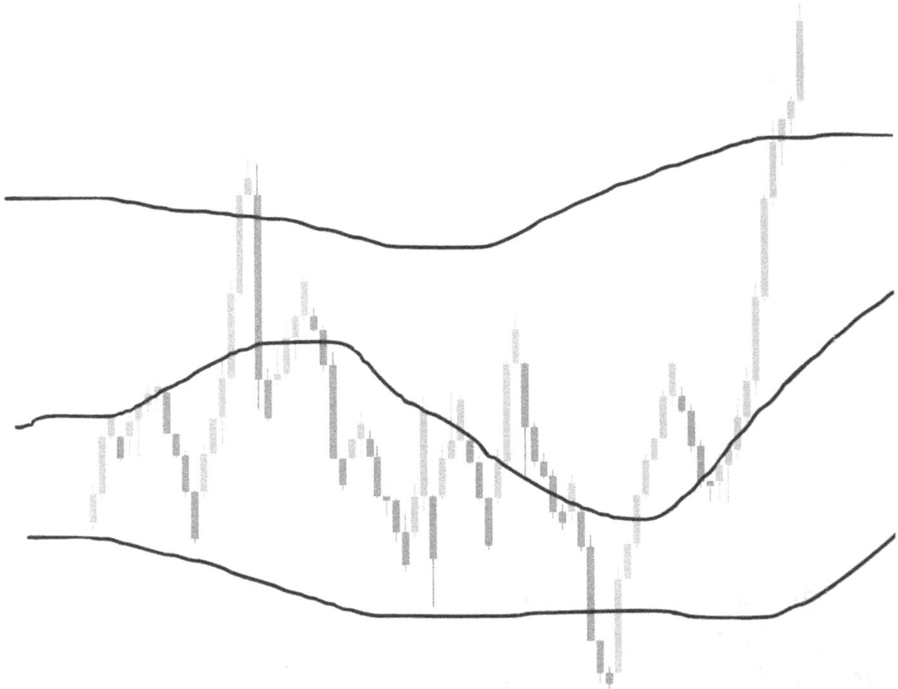

The **Middle Band** is a simple moving average (SMA), typically calculated over 20 periods. It represents the average price over a specified time frame.

The **Upper Band** is the middle band plus a specified number of standard deviations (usually two) of the price. It reflects the upper limit of the price range based on historical volatility.

The **Lower Band** is the middle band minus the same number of standard deviations as the upper band. It represents the lower limit of the price range.

How They Work

Volatility Measure: When the market is more volatile, the bands widen as the standard deviation increases. When volatility is low, the bands contract.

Price Action Analysis: Prices tend to move within the bands, and they often "bounce" off the upper or lower bands, returning toward the middle band. If prices consistently close outside the bands, it may indicate a strong trend in that direction.

Potential Signals

- **Overbought/Oversold Conditions**: Prices near the upper band may suggest the asset is overbought, while prices near the lower band may suggest oversold conditions.
- **Breakout Signals**: A breakout beyond the bands can indicate the start of a strong trend.

Limitations

Bollinger Bands are not predictive indicators but reactive ones, reflecting past price data. They work best when combined with other technical indicators or analysis methods, as they can give false signals in choppy or sideways markets. Traders and analysts often use Bollinger Bands as part of a broader trading strategy to make informed decisions about entry and exit points.

2.8 Key Indicators and Metrics for Crypto Trading

Several other technical indicators are used by traders to assess market conditions, identify trends, and make predictions about future price movements. They are crucial for traders who rely on quantitative data rather than qualitative analysis.

Moving Averages (MA) and Their Variants

One of the most popular technical indicators in both traditional and cryptocurrency markets is the **moving average (MA)**. MAs smooth out price data over a set period, helping to identify the direction of a trend. The two primary types of moving averages are:

- **Simple Moving Average (SMA)**: The SMA calculates the average price over a specific number of periods. It is the most basic form of moving average and is widely used by traders.
- **Exponential Moving Average (EMA)**: The EMA gives more weight to recent price data, making it more responsive to price changes. Traders often use the EMA for its sensitivity to the latest market conditions.

The **Golden Cross** and **Death Cross** are two key signals based on moving averages. A Golden Cross occurs when a short-term MA crosses above a long-term MA, signaling a potential upward trend. Conversely, a Death Cross occurs when a short-term MA crosses below a long-term MA, indicating a potential downward trend.

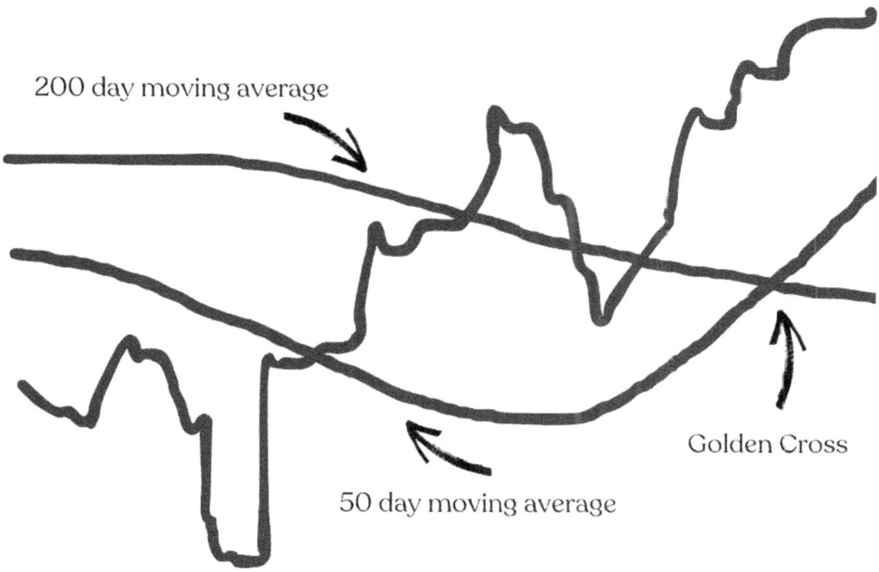
200 day moving average
Golden Cross
50 day moving average

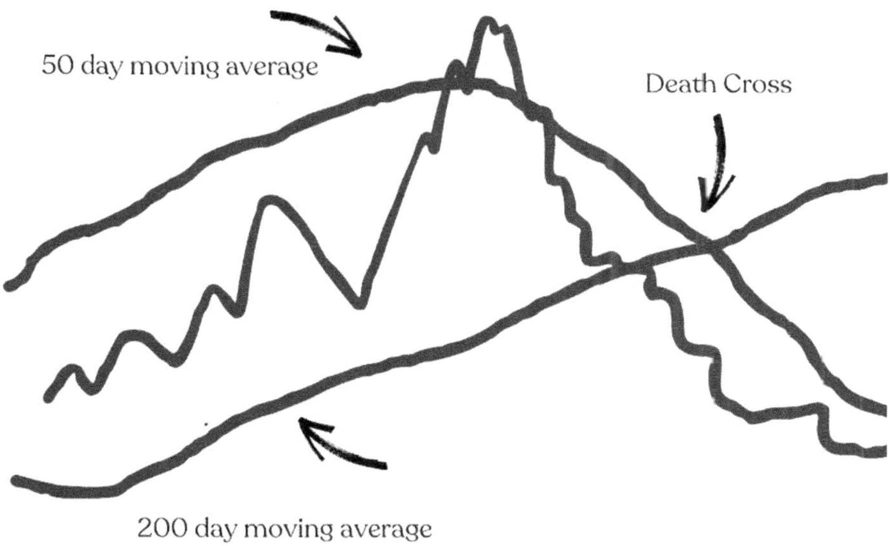
50 day moving average
Death Cross
200 day moving average

Relative Strength Index (RSI)

The **Relative Strength Index (RSI)** is a momentum oscillator used to identify overbought or oversold conditions in a market. This is a calculation that is obtained by comparing the average gains during a price increase to average losses during a time of price decrease. The specified amount of time is usually 14 days. RSI oscillates between 0 and 100 and helps determine whether a cryptocurrency is potentially overbought or oversold. An RSI above 70 indicates that the asset is overbought, which could suggest that a price reversal or pullback is imminent. An RSI below 30 indicates that the asset is oversold, potentially signaling a buying opportunity as the market may be due for a bounce.

MACD (Moving Average Convergence Divergence)

The **MACD** is another widely used technical indicator that helps identify changes in the strength, direction, momentum, and duration of a trend. The MACD is calculated by subtracting the 26-day Exponential Moving Average (EMA) from the 12-day EMA, and it is accompanied by a **signal line**, which is a 9-day EMA of the MACD. Traders look for **bullish crossovers** (when the MACD crosses above the signal line) and **bearish crossovers** (when the MACD crosses below the signal line) as potential buy and sell signals.

One of the simplest ways to keep track of these detailed types of indicators is to listen to analysis from experts in the field. Further in this book, I'll give some suggestions of methods you can use to follow market updates and analysis. For our purposes, I'm providing an overview so that when you hear market analysts talk about these indicators, you'll have a baseline understanding of what they're talking about. This understanding will also give you the background to know what to search for when seeking out analyst coverage. Had I known to look for these types of indicators in 2017, I would have made different trading decisions from the ones I made. Keep this section on hand to refer to when you hear analyses of market news. Then you can look up the terminology being used and better understand what the indicators being reported mean for the potential future direction of the market.

Volume Analysis and Its Importance

Volume is a critical metric for confirming price trends and understanding market sentiment. It refers to the number of units of a cryptocurrency that are traded over a given period. Volume can be used to confirm whether a trend is strong or weak. A price move accompanied by a high trading volume is often considered more reliable, while a price move with low volume may signal a lack of conviction.

Volume spikes often indicate a change in market sentiment and can signal an upcoming price breakout or reversal. For instance, an increase in volume during a **bullish breakout** can confirm that the trend is likely to continue, while a surge in volume during a **price decline** may indicate that a downtrend is gaining momentum.

Combining Indicators for Enhanced Analysis

While each indicator provides valuable insights, **combining multiple indicators** can lead to more reliable predictions. For example:

- **RSI + MACD**: When the RSI shows that an asset is oversold (below 30) and the MACD generates a bullish crossover, traders might take this as a stronger indication to buy.
- **Moving Averages + Bollinger Bands**: Bollinger Bands measure price volatility. By pairing a moving average with Bollinger Bands, traders can gain insight into whether the price is likely to continue moving in the direction of the trend or revert.

By combining multiple indicators, traders can reduce the risk of false signals and increase the reliability of their predictions. The most simplified way to keep up with these indicators is to subscribe to cryptocurrency newsletters and follow experts in the field who are adept at interpreting them. **In chapter 4, we'll take a look at some of the experts that could be worthwhile to follow.**

2.9 Conducting Fundamental Analysis on Cryptocurrencies

Fundamental analysis (FA) is another essential method for evaluating cryptocurrencies, with a focus on understanding a cryptocurrency's intrinsic value. While technical analysis is primarily concerned with historical price data, fundamental analysis examines the **underlying factors** that determine a cryptocurrency's long-term potential, such as its technology, use cases, and development team.

Assessing a Project's Underlying Technology

The **underlying technology** behind a cryptocurrency is important for determining its potential for long-term success. For example, **Ethereum**'s use of **smart contracts** enabled it to revolutionize the decentralized finance (DeFi) space. Evaluating the **blockchain's consensus mechanism** (such as proof-of-work or proof-of-stake) and whether it addresses scalability, security, and decentralization is an important step in understanding a cryptocurrency's long-term viability.

Evaluating Team Expertise and Project Vision

The **development team** is one of the most critical factors in determining a project's success. As noted already, a project with a strong, experienced team is more likely to deliver on its promises and avoid issues like **security vulnerabilities** or **lack of development progress**. Additionally, assessing the project's **vision** and whether it solves a real-world problem can provide significant insights into its potential for adoption.

Key Factors in Fundamental Analysis

In addition to the technology and team behind a project, several other **key factors** can affect a cryptocurrency's long-term viability:

- **Market Demand and Adoption Rates**: Adoption rate is the rate at which an asset is bought and embraced by the population. Cryptocurrencies with high adoption rates are more likely to succeed in the long term. For instance, **Bitcoin**'s status as the first and most widely adopted cryptocurrency has helped it maintain its dominant position in the market.
- **Competitive Landscape**: The cryptocurrency market is highly competitive. Projects that offer unique features, scalability, and usability often perform better. For instance, Cardano (ADA) and Polkadot (DOT) differentiate themselves from Ethereum by offering more scalable and energy-efficient blockchain solutions. Scalability is each currency's blockchain network's capability to handle increasing transactions without decreasing performance.

Analyzing a Cryptocurrency's Whitepaper

One of the first steps in research is to analyze a cryptocurrency's **whitepaper**. A whitepaper is the cornerstone of any cryptocurrency project, outlining its goals, technology, and economic model. When evaluating a cryptocurrency, it is essential to read and understand this document by its developers. This is especially important when evaluating new projects that may not yet have a proven track record. A well-written whitepaper should clearly articulate the problem the project aims to solve and how it intends to do so. A lack of clarity in the whitepaper may indicate a project with uncertain goals. The whitepaper should also demonstrate that the technology behind the project is viable. Overly ambitious or unrealistic claims without technical backing should raise concerns.

Equally important is evaluating the **team behind the cryptocurrency**. A strong team of experienced developers, advisors, and stakeholders increases the likelihood of a successful project. A well-rounded team can adapt to market changes, fix technical issues, and build a reputable project that has staying power. On the other hand, a team with little experience or a history of failed projects should raise a red flag. Remember that sometimes new cryptocurrencies are introduced into the market at fractions of a penny, only to be out of business within a year. So it takes more than just a low entry price to make a new cryptocurrency a good investment.

Case Studies of Successful Fundamental Analysis

Ethereum: Early investors in Ethereum recognized the potential of its smart contract technology, even before its launch. Ethereum's growth trajectory was driven by its ability to address the limitations of Bitcoin, particularly in terms of programmability and scalability.

Binance Coin (BNB): Binance Coin's early success was due in part to its utility within the Binance ecosystem. As Binance grew, so did BNB's use cases, driving its price upward. Fundamental analysis helped identify BNB's value as a utility token, leading to early investments.

2.10 Combining Technical and Fundamental Analysis for Optimal Results

Using both **technical analysis (TA)** and **fundamental analysis (FA)** provides a well-rounded approach to cryptocurrency trading. While technical analysis is useful for short-term decision-making, fundamental analysis helps evaluate the long-term potential of a cryptocurrency.

By combining both methods, traders can gain insights into both the short-term price movements and the long-term value of a cryptocurrency. TA can help identify ideal entry and exit points based on market sentiment and price trends, while FA can provide a broader context, ensuring that investments are made in fundamentally sound projects.

A practical strategy is to **use fundamental analysis to select promising cryptocurrencies** and then **use technical analysis to determine the best time to enter or exit a trade**. For instance, if a trader has identified a fundamentally strong project like Ethereum, they might use RSI or MACD to identify ideal buy and sell opportunities based on market conditions.

While combining both analyses is powerful, there can be challenges. **Conflicting signals** may arise when the technical analysis suggests one thing while the fundamental analysis suggests another. For example, a project may have a solid team and a strong foundation, but its market may stagnate. This happened with Bitcoin during its lengthy bear market in 2018 and 2019. Or alternatively, a currency may have a mediocre background but show great potential in the market. Tron (TRX) experienced this in late 2017 when its value jumped from 3 cents to 36 cents in a matter of hours, only to quickly fall again. However, despite its rapid fall, this cryptocurrency's fundamentals turned out to be stronger than it appeared to me 2017, as I'll touch on in the next paragraph. Balancing the short-term focus of technical analysis with the long-term focus of fundamental analysis can be difficult, but one strategy is to focus more on technical analysis for short-term trades and fundamental analysis for securing long-term holdings.

One pitfall to be aware of is a scheme called **pump and dump**. A pump and dump is an insider trading scheme that occurs when the market is manipulated in such a significant way that a mass amount of investors are lured into buying the asset through false advertising, causing the market for the asset to artificially and rapidly rise. When this occurs, new investors enter the market, trying to catch the wave of the bull run, but they unsuspectingly fall victim when the insiders causing the manipulation suddenly withdraw all their assets at the top price, causing the asset to crash and all of its followers to be left out. This appears to be what occurred with Tron (TRX) in 2017, when it soared in a matter of hours and just as suddenly came crashing down. However, it's important to note that while 36 cents was an extravagant pump for Tron in 2017, it's price in 2025 is almost that high naturally, indicating that it does have staying power in the market. Watching currencies elevate naturally over a course of time is a safer bet than seeing them shoot up inorganically. Bitcoin Cash (BCH) saw the same rapid rise and sudden fall in late 2017. Shiba Inu (SHIB) is also theorized to have experienced this manipulated cycle. These potential pump and dumps don't discredit the fundamental value of the currencies, but they are also not indicators of it and should not be used in either technical or fundamental analysis. If you do choose to jump on board a rapid pump, it's critical to keep a close eye on it and be prepared to jump out quickly. But keep in mind that insiders may all jump out in a moment with no warning, causing the value to crash before you can sell.

Alternatively, when following sustainable cryptocurrencies that have a natural, rhythmic ebb and flow, you can more safely implement a **"buy low/sell high"** strategy. An example is buying Bitcoin when it dips down to what experts consider the support level for its current cycle, and then selling it at the resistance level and waiting for the next support level to buy it again. This successful integration of both the technical and fundamental analyses of the Bitcoin market cycle helps traders capitalize on the technical volatility while also capitalizing on the broader long-term potential of Bitcoin as a store of value.

2.11 Media and Information Sites

Media outlets like CoinDesk and Cointelegraph play a vital role in shaping public perception and providing analysis of market trends. These platforms offer news, insights, and expert opinions on developments in the cryptocurrency world, which can help investors make informed decisions. They also cover regulatory changes, industry events, and the latest technological advancements. YouTube channel Altcoin Daily and newsletter The Block are also invaluable information sources.

Reddit and X serve as important forums for community-driven discussions and trends. Subreddits like r/CryptoCurrency are hubs for users to share news, analysis, and opinions, often influencing market sentiment. Social media has become a powerful tool for driving hype around particular coins, projects, or events, and platforms like X are frequently used by key figures in the crypto space to announce developments.

Social media has a profound impact on cryptocurrency trends and market behavior. **Viral trends** can quickly propel a cryptocurrency into the spotlight, as seen with Dogecoin (DOGE). Initially created as a joke, Dogecoin gained a massive following on Reddit and X, leading to significant price surges. Social media's ability to generate interest and create viral moments can have a direct impact on a cryptocurrency's value, sometimes causing dramatic price fluctuations based on public sentiment.

2.12 Setting Realistic Investment Goals with Cryptocurrencies

Setting clear, achievable investment goals is worthwhile for success in the cryptocurrency market. Without a clear plan, investors may fall prey to emotional decision-making and impulsive trades, which we'll explore in chapter 4. For now, let's talk about a framework for establishing realistic objectives and tips for tracking and adjusting goals.

Having well-defined goals helps investors remain focused and disciplined. Whether aiming for short-term gains or long-term wealth accumulation, clear goals give investors a roadmap for decision-making. Goals should align with an individual's risk tolerance, ensuring that expectations are realistic given the volatility of the market.

A structured approach to goal setting can increase the likelihood of success. One popular framework is the **SMART goals** system: Specific, Measurable, Achievable, Relevant, and Time-bound. For example, an investor might set a SMART goal to achieve a 10% return on their portfolio within one year by focusing on low-risk, high-cap cryptocurrencies.

Some common mistakes when setting investment goals include **overestimating potential returns** or failing to account for market volatility. Additionally, it is essential to remain **flexible** when adjusting goals based on changing market conditions. Unrealistic goals can lead to frustration and emotional decision-making, which should be avoided.

To track progress and adjust goals, investors can use performance metrics such as analyzing return on investment (ROI), portfolio growth, and risk-adjusted returns. Additionally, tools like portfolio tracking apps can help investors monitor performance in real-time, allowing them to adjust their strategies and goals as necessary.

* * *

In conclusion, the volatility of cryptocurrency markets is a defining characteristic. Cryptocurrencies are known for their rapid price fluctuations, driven by factors like market sentiment, news, and technological developments. While this volatility offers opportunities for profit, it also increases the risk of substantial losses. Successful investors must learn how to navigate volatility, understanding when to take profits, cut losses, and adjust their strategies. Both technical analysis and fundamental analysis are a vital part of portfolio management. While technical analysis gives investors information needed to make decisions about short-term phrases, fundamental analysis provides the data needed to determine a cryptocurrency's long-term value. By understanding these foundational concepts, crafting a diversified portfolio, managing risk, and setting clear goals, investors can make informed decisions and maximize their chances of success in the exciting world of cryptocurrency investing.

3

Chapter 3: Security Protocols for Safeguarding Digital Assets

3.1 Identifying and Avoiding Cryptocurrency Scams

As the cryptocurrency market has grown, so has the prevalence of scams and fraudulent schemes. These scams can take many forms, from fake initial coin offerings (ICOs) to Ponzi schemes. While we mentioned the pump and dump scheme in the previous chapter, in this section, we will explore other common types of cryptocurrency scams, how to spot them, and strategies for safeguarding against fraud.

Common Types of Cryptocurrency Scams

One of the most common types of scams in the crypto space is **phishing**. Phishing attacks typically involve fraudsters impersonating legitimate companies or individuals to steal sensitive information such as private keys or login credentials. Scammers may create fake websites or send phishing emails that appear to be from reputable cryptocurrency exchanges or wallet providers. To avoid phishing attacks, it is essential to verify the authenticity of websites and always check the URL for subtle changes that might indicate a fake site. A very common phishing scheme is phone calls from people claiming to be representatives of Coinbase or other exchanges, stating an account problem. I personally receive phone calls from Coinbase impersonators on a weekly basis. Coinbase states on its website that it does not call customers.

Another prevalent scam is the **Ponzi scheme**. In a Ponzi scheme, early investors are paid with the funds of newer investors, rather than from legitimate profits. Eventually, when the scheme can no longer attract new investors, it collapses, and the majority of investors lose their money. Ponzi schemes often promise high, guaranteed returns with little risk, which should serve as a red flag for potential investors.

Fake **ICOs** and token sales are also common scams. These schemes involve the launch of a new cryptocurrency project (initial coin offering) that promises high returns, but in reality, the project may have little to no viability. Unsuspecting investors may be lured into contributing funds to these projects, only to realize later that the project was a scam. To avoid falling for fake ICOs, investors should thoroughly research the project, its team, and the whitepaper before investing.

Verifying the Legitimacy of Crypto Projects

To avoid falling victim to scams, investors must conduct thorough **due diligence** before investing in any cryptocurrency project. Due diligence refers to the process of carefully researching and analyzing a cryptocurrency project before investing. This is done through thoroughly investigating the **feasibility**, **sustainability**, and **long-term potential** of potential investments. It involves evaluating the project's technology, business model, and market potential. Investors should also assess the project's **competitive positioning** within the broader cryptocurrency landscape.

When **checking the credentials of the team** behind the project, take note that reputable projects typically have experienced developers, industry experts, and advisors whose professional backgrounds can be verified. A lack of transparency regarding the team or an anonymous team behind a project is often a red flag.

Transparency is essential when evaluating crypto projects. Investors should ensure that the project provides **public audits** and **security certifications** from reputable third parties. Transparent projects will also have active **community-driven transparency initiatives**, such as regular updates, open-source code, and detailed financial reports.

In addition, while carefully reviewing the project's **whitepaper** and **roadmap**, be aware that the whitepaper should provide a clear explanation of the technology behind the project and its research. Reviewing the technology involves evaluating the **blockchain platform**, consensus mechanism, and any innovations that the project claims to have. Remember that a vague or poorly written whitepaper is often a sign of a scam. Additionally, the project's roadmap should outline the development milestones and timelines, helping investors gauge the project's feasibility and potential for success.

Several tools and resources can aid investors in their research. **Blockchain explorers** like Etherscan provide transaction histories and allow investors to track the progress of specific projects. Additionally, CoinMarketCap and CoinGecko offer valuable market data, including price trends, market capitalization, and trading volumes.

One of the best ways to stay up to date with what's happening in the crypto space is to pay attention to the buzz surrounding different currencies. If you follow online cryptocurrency groups and no one is talking about an initial coin offering, it may not be a viable project. Remember that staying informed through trusted **news sources** such as CoinDesk and CoinTelegraph can help investors avoid scams, as **third-party reviews** of crypto projects can help confirm their legitimacy. Think of the world of cryptocurrency as the wild west of the economy, ripe for exploring, but best explored with caution, and remember to stay connected to other travelers on this journey to help you navigate the wilderness.

Red Flags Indicating Potential Scams

One of the most significant warning signs is the promise of unrealistic returns. If a project promises guaranteed high returns with no risk, it is likely a scam. Similarly scams often avoid providing clear and verifiable details, making it difficult for investors to assess the legitimacy of the project.

3.2 Safeguarding Against Scams by Choosing Reputable Exchanges and Wallets

To protect against scams, investors should only use **reputable exchanges** and **wallet providers**. By choosing well-established platforms with strong security measures, investors reduce the risk of falling victim to fraud. The cryptocurrency space is still relatively young, and its history is filled with both remarkable successes and significant failures.

Real-World Examples of Exchange Failures and Successes

To better understand the importance of choosing the right exchange, let's look at some real-world examples of exchange failures and successes, as well as the lessons learned from these events.

The **Mt. Gox hack** is one of the most infamous incidents in cryptocurrency history. Mt. Gox, once the world's largest Bitcoin exchange, was hacked in 2014, resulting in the loss of approximately 850,000 Bitcoins, valued at over $450 million at the time. The exchange's lack of robust security measures, combined with inadequate management and transparency, led to its downfall and loss of customer funds. The Mt. Gox hack highlighted the importance of **security** in the crypto space and the need for exchanges to adopt robust measures to protect users' funds. For investors, this event underscored the importance of choosing exchanges with strong security measures and regulatory compliance.

Another notable failure was the **BitConnect Ponzi scheme**, which promised investors massive returns through a lending program. However, BitConnect collapsed in 2018, leaving many investors with worthless tokens. The BitConnect scandal serves as a cautionary tale about **high-risk, unregulated projects** that promise unrealistically high returns.

On the other hand, exchanges like Kraken have built a reputation for security and reliability. Kraken has a comprehensive set of security features, including two-factor authentication, encryption, and cold storage. The platform has never been hacked, and it has also gained regulatory approval in various jurisdictions. Kraken's transparency, commitment to customer service, and adherence to regulatory standards have helped it become one of the most trusted exchanges in the market.

Lessons Learned from Successful Recovery Efforts

While some projects have failed, others have shown resilience and the ability to recover from significant setbacks. For example, Binance successfully navigated multiple security breaches and hack attempts by implementing robust security protocols and transparent communication with users. Binance's response demonstrated the importance of **security enhancements** and **user trust** in rebuilding after a crisis.

Similarly, Ethereum successfully recovered from the **DAO hack** in 2016, when a vulnerability in the decentralized autonomous organization (DAO) led to the theft of millions of dollars' worth of Ether. The Ethereum community decided to **fork the blockchain** to reverse the effects of the hack. **Forking** is a process of splitting the currency into two different paths, often resulting in a change to the original protocol or the creation of a new version of the currency. This resilient act in Ethereum demonstrated the power of **community governance** in resolving issues and moving forward.

Key Takeaways for Future Investments

One of the key takeaways from these cases is the importance of **security**. Investors should prioritize projects that have strong security protocols in place, including regular audits and transparent development practices.

Additionally, **community involvement** in project governance is invaluable, as community-driven initiatives can help ensure transparency and accountability in the long run.

The failures and successes of the past have shaped the **current market practices** in the cryptocurrency space. After incidents like Mt. Gox and BitConnect, the crypto industry has become more aware of the need for **regulation**, **security enhancements**, and **investor education**. As a result, many exchanges and projects have adopted more stringent security measures, and investors are now more cautious when evaluating new ventures.

3.3 Understanding Cryptocurrency Wallets: Hot vs. Cold

Cryptocurrency wallets are digital tools used to store, send, and receive digital assets such as Bitcoin, Ethereum, and other cryptocurrencies. They function as the digital equivalent of a traditional bank account, allowing users to manage their assets securely. Remember that wallets operate through the use of cryptographic keys: **public keys**, which are used to receive funds, and **private keys**, which allow users to access and control their funds.

Functionality of Wallets in Sending and Receiving Cryptocurrencies

A cryptocurrency wallet enables users to interact with the blockchain. By generating public and private key pairs, wallets facilitate the secure transfer of digital assets. When a user wishes to send cryptocurrency, the wallet uses their **private key** to sign the transaction. This cryptographic signature verifies the sender's ownership and authorization of the funds, ensuring the security and legitimacy of the transaction.

Receiving cryptocurrencies is equally simple: users share their **public key** (which is often represented as an alphanumeric address) with the sender. This key allows the blockchain to direct the funds to the correct recipient. The wallet then stores the balance, and the user can monitor their transactions through the wallet interface.

Private keys are the most important security element in a cryptocurrency wallet. These keys are essentially passwords that grant access to the funds stored within the wallet. If a private key is compromised or lost, the funds are at risk, and there is no way to retrieve them. Hence, **private keys** must be safeguarded with the utmost care, typically stored offline and never shared with others.

Public keys, on the other hand, are designed to be shared. They serve as the destination address for receiving funds, and they don't carry the same security risks as private keys. However, public keys should still be handled with care to prevent any potential privacy leaks that might reveal sensitive transaction details.

Differences Between Hot and Cold Wallets

Cryptocurrency wallets can be broadly categorized into two types: **hot wallets** and **cold wallets**. The primary difference between the two is how they connect to the internet and the level of security they offer.

Hot Wallets for Convenience and Frequent Transactions

Hot wallets are connected to the internet, making them convenient for frequent trading or transactions. These wallets allow users to easily send and receive funds and manage their holdings through apps, websites, or software installed on their devices. Since they are always online, hot wallets are ideal for users who engage in day-to-day trading or wish to access their funds quickly.

Examples of popular hot wallets include MetaMask, a browser extension wallet primarily used for Ethereum-based tokens and decentralized applications (dApps), and Trust Wallet, a mobile wallet that supports a wide range of cryptocurrencies including Bitcoin, Ethereum, and many altcoins. The main advantage of hot wallets is their **accessibility** and **ease of use**, allowing quick transactions and portfolio management.

Cold Wallets for Enhanced Security and Long-Term Storage

Cold wallets, by contrast, are not connected to the internet. This makes them far more secure than hot wallets, as they are less vulnerable to hacking and malware attacks. Cold wallets are ideal for long-term storage of cryptocurrencies, where security is a higher priority than immediate accessibility. These wallets can take the form of **hardware wallets** or **paper wallets**, both of which store private keys offline.

Examples of cold wallets include Ledger Nano S/X and Trezor, two leading hardware wallet brands. These wallets use physical devices to store private keys, and the keys never leave the device itself, even during transactions. To complete a transaction, the user must physically connect the hardware wallet to their computer or mobile device and confirm the action on the wallet itself, ensuring that the private key remains secure. These two popular wallets have different functions that can appeal to different users' needs. Ledger Nano X is a hardware wallet that supports over 1,500 cryptocurrencies and has Bluetooth connectivity for mobile device use. Trezor Model T is another leading hardware wallet known for its security features, including a touch screen for easier navigation.

Pros and Cons of Each Wallet Type

Hot Wallets

Pros:

- **Convenience**: Hot wallets are perfect for users who need quick access to their funds for trading or other transactions.
- **Ease of Use**: They are often user-friendly and compatible with multiple devices, making them ideal for both beginners and experienced traders.
- **Instant Transactions**: Since hot wallets are always connected to the internet, transactions are fast and easy to execute.

Cons:

- **Vulnerability to Hacking**: Hot wallets are connected to the internet, which makes them more susceptible to cyber-attacks, phishing scams, and malware. If the private keys are compromised, users can lose their funds.
- **Less Security**: Although encryption and strong passwords provide a layer of protection, hot wallets can be compromised if the user's device or network is breached.

Cold Wallets

Pros:

- **Enhanced Security**: Cold wallets are offline, making them much less susceptible to hacking, malware, and other online threats. The private keys remain completely isolated from the internet, ensuring a higher level of security.
- **Ideal for Long-Term Storage**: Cold wallets are perfect for individuals who want to store large amounts of cryptocurrency securely for extended

periods.

- **Peace of Mind**: With cold wallets, users can rest assured that their assets are safe, provided they keep their backup keys and recovery phrases secure.

Cons:

- **Lack of Accessibility**: Cold wallets are not ideal for frequent transactions, as they require physical access to the device and some technical knowledge to use.
- **Potential Loss of Funds**: If users lose their cold wallet device or forget their backup phrase, they could permanently lose access to their funds, as there is no way to recover the private keys.

3.4 Setting Up Secure Wallets and Avoiding Common Pitfalls

Setting up a cryptocurrency wallet is a straightforward process, but it's important to follow best practices to ensure the security of your funds. Below is a step-by-step guide to setting up a secure wallet, as well as advice on avoiding common mistakes.

Step-by-Step Guide to Setting Up a Wallet

1. **Choose the Right Wallet**: Depending on your needs, decide whether a hot or cold wallet is best suited for you. Hot wallets are convenient for frequent transactions, while cold wallets provide enhanced security for long-term storage.
2. **Create a Strong Password**: When setting up a wallet, always use a strong, unique password. Avoid using common phrases or personal information that can be easily guessed.
3. **Enable Two-Factor Authentication (2FA)**: Whenever possible, enable

two-factor authentication (2FA) for an added layer of security. This typically involves using a mobile app (e.g., Google Authenticator or Authy) to generate a time-sensitive code in addition to your password.

4. **Backup Seed Phrases and Private Keys:** During the wallet setup, you will be provided with a **seed phrase** (a set of 12-24 words) and/or **private keys**. These are critical for recovering your wallet if your device is lost or damaged. Write down the seed phrase and store it in a safe location offline. Never store it digitally or online.
5. **Store Backup Securely:** Ensure that your backup information is stored in a secure location, such as a safe or a secure offline storage device. Never share your seed phrase or private keys with anyone.

Common Mistakes and How to Avoid Them

Storing Private Keys Online: Never store your private keys or seed phrases online or on cloud services, as these can be hacked. Always store this information offline in a secure, encrypted format.

Ignoring Software Updates: Keep your wallet software up to date to benefit from the latest security patches. Ignoring updates can expose your wallet to security vulnerabilities that hackers can exploit.

Reusing Passwords: Reusing passwords across different platforms increases the risk of a security breach. Always use unique passwords for each service, including your wallet.

Falling for Phishing Scams: Be cautious of emails, messages, phone calls or websites asking for your wallet details. Always double-check URLs and avoid clicking on suspicious links. You can also check your wallet's policies on contacting customers. If you believe your wallet provider has contacted you, go directly to the provider's website and place a support ticket instead of replying.

Importance of Regular Security Audits

It's crucial to regularly review your wallet's security settings and practices to ensure they remain up to date. Here's what to check periodically:

- **Check for Unauthorized Access**: Monitor your wallet activity for any unauthorized transactions or logins. Some wallets offer a history of activities or alerts if new devices attempt to access the wallet.

- **Update Security Measures**: As new threats emerge, update your security measures accordingly. This includes changing passwords, updating wallet software, or adopting additional layers of security like multi-signature authentication.

Best Practices for Wallet Management

Use Hardware Wallets for Large Holdings: For large amounts of cryptocurrency, use a cold hardware wallet to ensure enhanced security. Use hot wallets for currencies you intend to trade in the near future.

Regularly Change Passwords and Access Codes: Change your wallet password and access codes periodically to ensure your funds remain secure, especially if you suspect your device or login credentials may have been compromised.

3.5 Advanced Security Measures: Encryption Techniques

As cryptocurrencies are inherently digital, they rely heavily on encryption to protect transactions and stored assets. Let's dive into some advanced encryption techniques that enhance the security of digital wallets.

Data Encryption Standards (AES, RSA)

AES (Advanced Encryption Standard) is one of the most widely used encryption algorithms, providing strong protection for sensitive data. It's used by many cryptocurrency wallets to encrypt private keys and transaction data, ensuring that even if a hacker gains access to your wallet, they won't be able to read or alter your assets without the proper decryption key.

RSA Encryption (Rivest-Shamir-Adleman) is an asymmetric encryption algorithm that uses a public-private key pair for secure data transmission. It's often used in conjunction with other encryption methods to ensure the security of wallets and cryptocurrency transactions.

End-to-End Encryption for Secure Messaging: Many wallet providers and cryptocurrency platforms implement **end-to-end encryption** (E2EE) to secure communications between users. This ensures that only the sender and recipient can read the messages, making it difficult for hackers or third parties to intercept sensitive information.

Multi-Signature Wallets

A **multi-signature (multi-sig)** wallet requires more than one private key to authorize a transaction. This adds an extra layer of protection, ensuring that even if one private key is compromised, the funds remain safe unless additional keys are also compromised.

Cryptographic Hash Functions: SHA-256 in Bitcoin

Cryptographic hash functions like **SHA-256** (used in Bitcoin) are integral to securing transactions and verifying the integrity of blockchain data. Hash functions take input data and produce a fixed-length, unique output, ensuring that data cannot be tampered with once it's recorded on the blockchain.

3.6 Protecting Your Digital Identity in the Crypto World

In the digital economy, **protecting your digital identity** is just as important as safeguarding your physical identity. Cybersecurity threats such as **identity theft** and **fraud** are prevalent in the crypto world, and the importance of protecting your personal information cannot be overstated for maintaining financial security.

Methods for Enhancing Digital Identity Security

Use VPNs for Secure Internet Connections: A **VPN (Virtual Private Network)** encrypts your internet connection, ensuring that your online activities remain private. This is especially important when conducting cryptocurrency transactions, as it prevents third parties from intercepting your communications.

Employ Privacy-Focused Browsers: Browsers like Tor and privacy-focused extensions like Privacy Badger can help protect your identity and ensure that your browsing history is kept private.

Role of Anonymity in Cryptocurrency Transactions

Cryptocurrencies like Monero and Zcash focus on privacy, using advanced encryption methods to provide **anonymity** for transactions. While this protects users from surveillance and tracking, it also presents challenges for law enforcement and regulatory bodies.

Safe Online Behavior Tips

Avoid Public Wi-Fi: Never conduct sensitive transactions, such as cryptocurrency trades, over public Wi-Fi networks, as these are often insecure and vulnerable to hackers.

Recognize Phishing Attempts: In addition to always verifying the legitimacy of emails, messages, or websites requesting wallet information, remember to also avoid clicking on links from unknown sources.

3.7 Lessons Learned from Past Security Breaches

The Mt. Gox hack and DAO attack on Ethereum highlighted the need for **decentralized security measures**, better smart contract audits, and improved exchange security protocols. In response, the industry has adopted stronger security practices. In addition to the use of **multi-signature technology** and **secure hardware wallets** following these breaches, cryptocurrency exchanges and wallet providers have also focused on enhancing transparency and accountability, implementing regular security audits, and adopting decentralized security frameworks to minimize risks.

To avoid similar breaches, exchanges and organizations should **conduct regular security audits** and **implement incident response plans**. As the investor, you'll want to ensure that wallet and exchange systems undergo thorough security audits to identify vulnerabilities. You'll also want to make sure they prepare for potential breaches by having a clear incident response plan in place that includes backup strategies and recovery procedures.

* * *

By understanding the causes of volatility, implementing sound risk management practices, and learning from past mistakes, investors can make informed decisions and protect their investments in the unpredictable world of cryptocurrency. This chapter has provided a comprehensive overview of **cryptocurrency wallets** and **security best practices**, offering both theoretical and practical knowledge to help users safeguard their digital assets. From understanding the difference between hot and cold wallets to implementing advanced encryption measures and securing your digital identity, this information empowers readers to navigate the crypto landscape confidently and securely.

* * *

Make a Difference with Your Review

Unlock the Power of Generosity

"Knowledge grows when shared, and wisdom lights the way for others."

Imagine helping someone just like you—curious about cryptocurrency trading but unsure where to begin.

My mission is simple: to make cryptocurrency trading easy to understand and fun to explore for everyone. This book is designed to guide beginners through the basics, helping them build a strong foundation to trade confidently.

But to reach more people and make an even bigger impact, I need your help. Most people pick books based on reviews. By leaving a review, you're not just sharing your thoughts—you're helping someone take their first step into the world of cryptocurrency.

It costs nothing and takes just a minute of your time, but your words could:

- Help a new trader find a book that makes tricky concepts clear.
- Save someone from falling for common crypto scams.
- Empower families to make smart trading decisions and improve their financial future.
- Steer a beginner away from costly mistakes.
- Spark another crypto success story!

Your review might be the encouragement someone needs to start their journey.

To make a difference, simply scan the QR code below and leave a review:

Thank you for being part of this mission to make cryptocurrency trading accessible and enjoyable for all. Your voice matters, and your generosity could inspire others to take that important first step.

Let's grow the crypto community—together!

4

Chapter 4: Psychological Aspects of Trading and Getting Support

4.1 The Psychology of Trading: Overcoming Fear and Greed

While cryptocurrency offers exciting investment opportunities, it is also fraught with risks. Many investors fall into common pitfalls that can negatively impact their returns. **Overtrading** is one such mistake. The highly volatile nature of the cryptocurrency market can be tempting, and it may lead some investors to constantly buy and sell assets in an attempt to profit from short-term price fluctuations. However, overtrading often results in significant transaction fees and missed opportunities. It can also cause emotional strain, which leads to poor decision-making.

Emotional decision-making is a dangerous trap. Cryptocurrencies are notoriously volatile, and market swings can trigger strong emotional responses such as fear, greed, or FOMO (fear of missing out). These emotions often lead investors to make irrational decisions. **Fear** and **greed,** two of the most powerful and common emotions, often drive traders to make irrational and costly choices. When fear and greed lead to panic, it often in turn leads to impulsive decisions, such as selling during a market dip or buying based on hype. They can also trigger other irrational decisions, such as over-leveraging, or holding onto a losing position for too long.

Emotional discipline is one of the biggest challenges in cryptocurrency trading. In the volatile world of trading, emotions play a pivotal role in shaping decision-making processes. Understanding these emotions, recognizing when they take hold, and knowing how to mitigate their influence can significantly improve a trader's success. Successful traders must learn to manage their emotions and stick to a well-thought-out strategy that aligns with their long-term goals.

Fear-Induced Selling During Market Downturns

Fear is one of the most destructive emotions in trading. A common symptom of fear is panic selling. When the market experiences a downturn and traders see their investments start to lose value, fear often causes them to panic and instinctively sell their positions in haste to prevent further losses. However, this knee-jerk reaction often happens too early, before the market has had a chance to rebound. The result is traders exiting positions prematurely, locking in losses. This behavior can be especially prevalent during short-term volatility when the market dips but eventually recovers. Fear-induced selling can cause further declines in asset prices, as more and more people join in panic selling, creating a cycle that continues to exacerbate the downward spiral.

For instance, during the **2020 market crash**, many investors were terrified by the rapid and unpredictable decline in global markets. This widespread panic led to mass sell-offs, causing prices to drop even further than necessary. Fear-based selling can cause traders to miss out on potential recoveries, as markets tend to rebound after a downturn.

Greedy Over-Leveraging During Bull Markets

On the opposite end of the emotional spectrum is greed, which is particularly evident during bull markets. When markets are on an upward trajectory, greed drives traders to make excessively risky investments, believing that they will continue to rise indefinitely. This results in **over-leveraging**, where traders borrow large amounts of money to amplify potential profits. While this can lead to significant gains during a bull market, it also dramatically increases the risk of catastrophic losses when the market eventually corrects.

Greed also manifests in the belief that a losing position will eventually rebound. Traders may refuse to cut their losses and continue holding onto a position, hoping for a recovery. This emotional attachment to a trade can prevent traders from accepting reality and moving on. The longer traders hold onto losing positions, the deeper their losses can become, and the harder it is to make rational decisions. Again, understanding the long-term potential for particular currencies goes a long way in helping investors make decisions that will benefit them.

For example, during the **2017 cryptocurrency boom**, many traders over-leveraged by borrowing funds to invest in Bitcoin and other altcoins. When the market turned, these traders faced severe losses, as their positions were liquidated due to margin calls. Greed clouds judgment, making traders more prone to taking risks without fully understanding the consequences.

Recognizing when fear or greed is influencing decisions is important for any trader. These emotions manifest in specific behaviors that, when identified, can help traders regain control and make more productive choices.

4.2 Strategies to Mitigate Fear and Greed

Fortunately, there are several practical strategies that traders can use to minimize the influence of these emotions. One common method is to establish clear **trading rules** and follow them rigorously. For example, traders can set predetermined entry and exit points and avoid making decisions based on short-term market movements. Additionally, traders can practice **mindfulness and self-awareness** to recognize emotional triggers and avoid impulsive actions. By staying calm and focused, traders can make more rational decisions and improve their chances of success in volatile markets.

Setting Predefined Entry and Exit Points

One of the most effective ways to combat fear and greed is by setting **predefined entry and exit points**. A well-thought-out trading plan ensures that traders do not react impulsively based on emotional impulses. By setting clear levels for **stop-loss** and **take-profit orders**, traders can automatically execute trades when their predetermined criteria are met, regardless of emotional influence. This allows for more disciplined and rational decision-making, preventing emotional overreaction.

Implementing a Cooling-Off Period Before Decision-Making

Another useful strategy is implementing a **cooling-off period** before making any major trading decisions. If emotions are running high—whether it's due to a sudden loss or a rapid price increase—taking a break can help clear the mind and avoid impulsive decisions. Stepping away from the trading screen and engaging in an activity that relaxes the mind, such as reading or walking, can help reduce the impact of fear and greed.

Developing a Disciplined Trading Mindset

In addition to managing emotions, developing a **disciplined mindset** is essential for long-term success in trading. Discipline involves adhering to a well-structured plan, avoiding impulsive actions, and consistently applying proven strategies. A disciplined trader is focused, patient, and able to stick to their goals despite market fluctuations.

Characteristics of a Disciplined Trader

A disciplined trader possesses several key traits that contribute to consistent success:

Patience and the Ability to Wait for the Right Opportunities

Patience is one of the most important characteristics of a disciplined trader. Rather than jumping into trades at the first sign of market movement, disciplined traders wait for the right opportunities that align with their strategy. They understand that trading is a marathon, not a sprint, and they are willing to wait for favorable setups rather than forcing trades out of impatience.

Adherence to a Predetermined Trading Plan

A disciplined trader is one who adheres to a **predetermined trading plan**, which outlines specific goals, risk management rules, and entry and exit strategies. By following the plan, traders avoid the temptation to make emotional decisions or deviate from their strategy in the heat of the moment. A trading plan provides structure and consistency, allowing traders to stay focused on their objectives.

The Importance of Consistency in Trading

Consistency is key to becoming a successful trader. Inconsistent behavior—such as frequently changing strategies, abandoning risk management principles, or impulsively entering and exiting trades—can lead to losses and frustration. By applying a consistent approach, traders increase their chances of achieving long-term success.

Following a Routine to Eliminate Impulsive Decisions

One way to achieve consistency is by following a routine. By sticking to a daily or weekly routine, traders can eliminate the uncertainty that often leads to impulsive decisions. A routine might include analyzing the market at specific times, reviewing trade setups, and practicing risk management strategies. This structure helps traders maintain a balanced approach to their trading activities.

Consistent Application of Risk Management Techniques

Risk management is a core component of consistency in trading. Successful traders consistently apply risk management techniques, such as setting stop-loss orders and determining position sizes based on risk tolerance. By protecting capital and managing risk on every trade, traders reduce the likelihood of large losses that can destabilize their trading account.

Techniques for Building Trading Discipline

Developing discipline in trading requires consistent practice and a structured approach. Below are several techniques to help traders cultivate the discipline needed for long-term success:

Reviewing Trades Regularly to Identify Patterns and Areas for Improvement

Discipline is built over time by reflecting on past trades. Regularly reviewing trades allows traders to identify patterns in their decision-making process and assess whether they followed their strategy. This self-assessment helps to identify strengths and weaknesses, allowing traders to continuously improve their approach.

Alternatively, Refraining from Reviewing Trades in Order to Allow the Market to Correct Itself

For traders who become anxious when reviewing their trades and have difficulty refraining from overtrading, an alternative strategy is to simply put the wallet away for a while and come back to it much later to see what happens. This is effective for traders who have thoroughly researched the assets and are confident they have made good long-term investments. It can be rewarding to check on trades after six months or a year and see the long-term growth that has occurred. In this way, assets that are not growing can be reevaluated at that time with sufficient long-term data to make informed decisions.

Self-Reflection and Analyzing Past Trades to Learn from Mistakes

Self-reflection and continuous improvement are key aspects of successful trading. By regularly evaluating their performance and making adjustments to their strategies, traders can learn from past mistakes and become more effective over time. Traders should always take time to analyze their past trades to understand what worked and what didn't. This reflection process helps traders identify areas where they deviated from their plan, over-leveraged, or made impulsive decisions. By learning from mistakes, traders can refine their strategies and avoid repeating errors in the future.

Setting Personal Development Goals in Trading

Setting **personal development goals** is an essential part of continuous improvement. These goals may include improving technical analysis skills, learning new trading strategies, or managing emotions more effectively. By setting clear and achievable goals, traders can measure their progress and stay motivated on their trading journey.

4.3 The Role of a Balanced Lifestyle in Emotional Resilience

Maintaining a balanced lifestyle is essential for emotional resilience in trading. A healthy body and mind are better equipped to handle the stresses of the market. Physical health plays a key role in emotional well-being. **Regular exercise** boosts mood and reduces stress, while **proper nutrition** helps maintain energy levels and focus. A healthy body contributes to a clear mind, which is important for managing emotions while trading. **Adequate** sleep **and effective stress management practices**, such as relaxation techniques or hobbies, are also vital for emotional regulation. Poor sleep and chronic stress can impair cognitive function, leading to poor decision-making in trading.

The Role of Mindfulness in Emotional Regulation

Mindfulness is the practice of being fully present in the moment without judgment. It plays an important role in managing the emotions that influence trading decisions. By developing a mindful approach to trading, individuals can better control their emotional responses, leading to more rational decision-making.

Meditation and **breathing exercises** are powerful tools for reducing stress and promoting emotional balance. By dedicating just a few minutes a day to practicing deep breathing or guided meditation, traders can develop greater emotional awareness and gain better control over fear and greed. These practices help clear the mind, reduce anxiety, and promote calmness—especially in high-pressure trading environments.

Journaling is another effective mindfulness tool. By keeping a trading journal, traders can track not only their trades but also the emotional triggers that influenced their decisions. Writing down thoughts and feelings during trading sessions helps to bring awareness to patterns of emotional behavior, such as fear-driven selling or greed-fueled over-leveraging. This self-awareness can lead to more conscious decision-making in the future.

While keeping a **trading journal** is a valuable tool for building discipline, a trading journal tracks more than just emotional states during trades. By documenting trades, strategies, emotional triggers, and outcomes, traders can reflect on their decision-making process and identify areas for improvement. This practice encourages traders to stay focused on their goals and avoid making impulsive decisions based on emotions. It also provides valuable information for recalling the history of trades and assets. This is beneficial for the review process that we looked at earlier in this chapter and may come in handy when we get to tax implications in chapter 6.

Real-Life Examples of Emotional Management

Real-life examples of emotional management in practice demonstrate the importance of controlling fear and greed.

A Trader Avoiding Panic During Market Crashes

During the 2020 market crash, one trader, much like myself, stuck to their strategy by not panicking and selling their positions at a loss. Instead, they used stop-loss orders to manage risk and stayed calm. This approach allowed them to avoid locking in unnecessary losses and they ultimately benefited from the market's recovery.

Staying Composed and Making Rational Decisions During Volatile Periods

Another trader, during the cryptocurrency boom, avoided the temptation to over-leverage during the bull market. Unlike myself at the time, who didn't know about these strategies, they stuck to their risk management plan and gradually accumulated positions, ensuring that they were not caught in the frenzy of greed-driven decisions. As a result, they were able to weather the market correction with minimal losses and a disciplined approach.

4.4 Building Confidence Through Education and Practice

Confidence is a valuable component of successful trading. A trader who feels confident in their abilities is better equipped to navigate challenges and make decisions in high-pressure situations. Continuous education and practice are key to building this confidence. Learning is a lifelong journey in trading. Markets evolve, new tools emerge, and trading strategies change over time. Traders must continuously educate themselves to stay ahead.

Techniques for Effective Learning and Skill Development

Building trading skills requires a structured approach to learning. Traders should set clear learning goals, such as mastering technical analysis or improving emotional regulation, and track their progress over time. By breaking down learning objectives into manageable steps, traders can maintain focus and stay motivated. Further, engaging with trading communities allows traders to share experiences, learn from others, and gain insights into new strategies and tools. Joining forums, discussion groups, or social media platforms dedicated to trading can help expand knowledge and boost confidence.

Collaborative Learning: Workshops and Online Courses

Webinars and workshops offer great opportunities for traders to gain insights from experts, learn new strategies, and deepen their understanding of market dynamics. Attending these events helps traders **stay updated and improves their decision-making skills.**

The Value of Collaborative Learning in Crypto

Peer-to-Peer Knowledge Sharing: Collaborative learning enables knowledge to be shared among peers. Whether through group discussions or interactive workshops, participants learn from each other's experiences, creating a **collective knowledge base** that benefits everyone involved.

Group Projects and Interactive Sessions: Workshops and courses often include group projects where participants work together to solve real-world problems. This collaborative approach mimics the type of teamwork seen in blockchain development and project creation, offering students a taste of **real-world crypto application**.

Available Workshops and Online Courses

Online Platforms Like Coursera and Udemy: Both platforms offer numerous courses on cryptocurrency and blockchain technology. These courses range from introductory lessons to advanced trading strategies, allowing traders to gain a solid foundation in the space.

Workshops Hosted by Blockchain Organizations: Many blockchain companies and crypto organizations host educational workshops aimed at helping newcomers understand how crypto works. These events often feature hands-on training and the opportunity to ask questions directly from industry experts.

The benefits of collaborative learning environments are many. Group learning provides access to multiple ways of approaching problems. In the world of crypto trading, this is invaluable as traders must constantly adapt to new market conditions. This type of learning also provides networking opportunities with fellow learners. Participating in group learning environments allows you to meet others who share your interest in cryptocurrency. Many lifelong partnerships and collaborations have started in these types of learning spaces.

Reading Trading-Related Literature and Market Analyses

Reading books, articles, and market analyses is essential for broadening a trader's knowledge base. Understanding market theories, new technologies, and trading psychology contributes to greater confidence and competence. Coindesk and Cointelegraph, mentioned earlier, are two platforms that are widely regarded as reliable sources of news related to cryptocurrency. They cover breaking stories, in-depth analyses, and market insights to keep traders informed. **Market Analysis** from platforms like Glassnode and CryptoQuant offer on-chain analysis and data-driven insights into market trends, helping traders make more informed decisions. To manage the overwhelming amount of information, traders can use tools like **RSS feeds** or **news aggregators** that pull together the most relevant news stories into a single, easily digestible format.

Major Players in the Cryptocurrency Space

The cryptocurrency ecosystem is vast and continues to evolve rapidly. Several key players, platforms, and services shape the landscape, offering support for users and businesses involved in crypto. Understanding these entities can help you navigate the crypto world more effectively.

Cryptocurrency Developers and Innovators are at the forefront of the crypto industry, developing the technologies and protocols that drive innovation. Prominent developers include Vitalik Buterin, the creator of Ethereum, and Satoshi Nakamoto, the mysterious founder of Bitcoin. These innovators are responsible for pushing the boundaries of what is possible within blockchain technology and have shaped the direction of the entire industry.

Influential Investors and Venture Capitalists also play a vital role in the cryptocurrency ecosystem. High-profile investors like Tim Draper, Michael Saylor, and Andreessen Horowitz have backed various blockchain and crypto projects, helping to secure funding and legitimacy. These investors often have a significant influence on the direction of the industry, as their financial support can drive the development and adoption of new technologies.

Social media platforms like X and YouTube are home to crypto influencers who provide **insights**, **predictions**, and **analysis**. By following these trusted voices, traders can stay up-to-date with the latest developments.

Regulatory Bodies are another important player in the crypto space. Governments and regulatory agencies around the world are developing frameworks for regulating cryptocurrencies and blockchain technology. These bodies are shaping the legal landscape for cryptocurrencies, which can significantly impact the industry's growth and adoption. Subscribing to news and updates from key players in the ecosystem can help investors stay abreast of trends.

The Role of Practice in Building Trading Skills

Knowledge without practice can't be fully realized. **Practicing trading strategies in real-world conditions** is essential for developing skill and confidence. Demo accounts, mentioned earlier, are a great way to practice trading without risking real capital. By using these accounts, traders can simulate different market scenarios and test new strategies without the pressure of real-money losses. Another effective way to practice trading is by reviewing **historical data** and conducting technical analysis on past market movements. This helps traders develop an understanding of market patterns and become more proficient in identifying entry and exit points.

The Importance of Community in Crypto Trading

The cryptocurrency market is unique in its rapid pace, volatility, and ever-changing trends. This creates a landscape that can be intimidating and challenging for newcomers, as well as for seasoned traders. However, one of the greatest strengths of the crypto world is the sense of **community** that exists within it. Communities in the crypto ecosystem play an integral role in helping individuals navigate the complexities of cryptocurrency trading, providing a support system that is vital for success.

Communities in crypto can provide both **insightful information** and **emotional support**, both of which are essential in an industry marked by rapid fluctuations in price and sentiment. Given the vast amounts of information available, it's often the shared wisdom and experiences of community members that help traders make informed decisions.

Being actively engaged in a crypto community brings several benefits, particularly for traders looking to **improve their skills** and **navigate the volatile landscape**.

- **Access to Timely Information and Trends**: The cryptocurrency market operates around the clock, and the speed at which information travels can be both a blessing and a curse. Community engagement ensures that traders are not left in the dark, especially when sudden changes occur. By participating in online forums, groups, and social media channels, traders can gain access to **real-time information** about market trends, new coins, updates on blockchain technology, and even rumors that might affect price movement. Having a trusted group of people to help filter out noise and provide relevant news is invaluable in such a fast-moving market.
- **Sharing of Experiences and Strategies**: One of the primary benefits of being part of a crypto community is the **exchange of knowledge**. Members of a community often share their experiences—both successful and unsuccessful—about various strategies, trades, and market conditions. For example, experienced traders might offer insights on how they navigated certain bear markets or how they profited during periods of high volatility. Newer traders can learn from the mistakes and successes of others, thus avoiding common pitfalls.
- **Collective Problem-Solving and Innovation**: In the crypto world, problems such as **security issues**, **market crashes**, or even **regulatory changes** can arise unexpectedly. Communities often engage in collaborative problem-solving, leveraging the collective knowledge of their members to find innovative solutions. For example, when

a cryptocurrency exchange is hacked or when new regulations are introduced in a country, a community can quickly disseminate crucial information and discuss how these events might affect the market. This sense of collective problem-solving can help traders stay ahead of the curve and adapt their strategies accordingly.

- **Emotional Support During Market Volatility**: The emotional roller-coaster of the crypto market can lead to **fear**, **panic selling**, or **greed-fueled decisions** during bull runs. A well-formed community can provide emotional support, helping traders stay calm and stick to their plans. Having a space to discuss anxieties, vent frustrations, or celebrate wins with others who understand the challenges of crypto trading can be crucial for mental well-being. Communities also provide a sense of **belonging**, which can motivate traders to keep going through difficult periods.
- **Group Discussions and Brainstorming Sessions**: Crypto communities, whether they're hosted on platforms like Reddit or Discord, often organize group discussions, **AMA (Ask Me Anything)** sessions with industry experts, or brainstorming sessions. These discussions can lead to insights that members might not have come to on their own. For example, when a new blockchain upgrade or token listing is imminent, members can collaborate on understanding its potential impact. These brainstorming sessions can create an environment where individuals bring together diverse viewpoints, helping everyone arrive at a more nuanced understanding of market movements.
- **Open-Source Projects and Contributions**: Many crypto projects are built on open-source platforms, and communities often collaborate on the development of these projects. Open-source contributions allow community members to not only **learn** about the project but also **directly participate** in its growth. For instance, projects like Bitcoin and Ethereum have extensive open-source communities that allow developers to submit code changes, suggest improvements, and help troubleshoot problems. Being involved in open-source projects can offer traders a deeper understanding of the technologies behind crypto.

In the cryptocurrency ecosystem, **collaboration** and **learning** are often at the heart of success. The best crypto traders know that they are not alone, and that collaboration can make them better.

Examples of Reputable Crypto Communities

Several **well-established crypto communities** offer invaluable resources, knowledge, and support to traders and investors. These communities include both **social media groups** and **forum-based** platforms where people can ask questions, share experiences, and receive valuable guidance.

BitcoinTalk Forum: The BitcoinTalk forum, one of the oldest and most established communities in the cryptocurrency space, is where traders and developers from around the world converge to discuss all things related to Bitcoin, altcoins, and blockchain technology. The forum is divided into different sections, including **technical discussions**, **market analysis**, and **project development**. It remains a hub for these types of discussions, and it is often the first place where new ideas are proposed. Further, it's home to developers, miners, traders, and investors alike.

r/CryptoCurrency on Reddit: This subreddit is one of the largest communities focused on cryptocurrency, and it serves as an essential resource for traders looking to stay informed about the latest trends. Members share news, price analysis, and even personal stories about their experiences in crypto. Discussions often range from **technical analysis** to **investment strategies** to **scam alerts**.

Telegram and Discord Groups for Specific Projects and Real-Time Updates: Many crypto communities have shifted to real-time communication platforms like Telegram and Discord, which are widely used by crypto communities because of their real-time communication capabilities. These channels provide instant updates on market movements, new projects, and relevant news, making them an essential tool for staying informed in the fast-moving world of crypto. Many **ICO projects**, **token creators**, and **blockchain innovators** host Telegram groups for their supporters. These groups can offer timely updates, **networking opportunities**, and access to **exclusive content** such as live discussions and Q&A sessions with project developers.

Tips for Effective Networking in Crypto Forums

- **Joining Topic-Specific Threads and Discussions**: Start by joining conversations that match your interests and knowledge level. By contributing to discussions where you can add value, you'll establish yourself as a credible and valuable member of the community.
- **Reaching Out to Individuals with Similar Interests**: Don't hesitate to **direct message** or **network** with individuals who share your interests. This can lead to **partnerships** or **mentor-mentee relationships** that might accelerate your learning process.

Benefits of Active Participation

- **Learning from Diverse Perspectives**: One of the biggest advantages of being active in crypto forums is the ability to hear from a **diverse range of voices**. Different members may have different strategies, backgrounds, and experiences, offering you new perspectives on how to approach trading.
- **Building a Reputation and Credibility**: Active participation in forums allows you to **build a reputation** as a knowledgeable and reliable member. Over time, this can lead to opportunities for collaboration, mentorship, or even job offers within the crypto industry.

Etiquette and Best Practices for Forum Participation

- **Respectful Communication and Constructive Feedback**: When participating in forums, it's essential to communicate respectfully and offer constructive feedback. In online communities, disagreements can escalate quickly if members are disrespectful. Remember, the goal is to **learn** from others and **share** knowledge, not to engage in heated arguments.
- **Avoiding Spam and Self-Promotion**: To maintain the integrity of forums, avoid posting irrelevant content or overly promotional material. While sharing your own experiences and success stories is valuable, **self-promotion** can undermine the collaborative environment of a community.

Being part of a supportive **trading community** can also boost confidence. By exchanging ideas and receiving feedback from peers, traders can refine their strategies and gain motivation to keep improving.

Mentorship and Peer Support

Mentorship and peer support play a significant role in building confidence and skill in trading. The technology required to carry out trades comes with a steep learning curve, so having mentors who have been down the path and can answer questions can be a lifesaver in helping prevent costly trial and error mistakes. A mentor can provide valuable guidance and feedback, helping traders navigate the complexities of the market. A mentor's experience and advice can help new traders avoid common pitfalls and improve their strategies.

In any field, mentorship accelerates learning, and crypto trading is no exception. Having a mentor—an experienced trader or professional who offers **guidance** and **insight**—can make all the difference between success and failure.

The Importance of Mentorship in Crypto Trading

Personalized Advice and Feedback: Mentors offer personalized feedback and tailored advice to help you improve your trading skills. Whether it's refining your technical analysis, discussing entry and exit strategies, or providing a better understanding of market cycles, a mentor can significantly speed up the learning process. Having someone who has navigated the challenges of crypto trading can give you **confidence** in your decisions and **clarity** in your trading strategy.

Motivation and Encouragement from Experienced Traders: Mentors often serve as both **coaches** and **motivators**. Crypto markets can be tough and unforgiving, especially during bear markets. A mentor can offer encouragement during difficult times, reminding you to stick to your strategy and avoid emotional decision-making. Their experience helps you navigate the uncertainty with greater assurance.

Strategies for Identifying Potential Mentors

Finding a reliable mentor can be difficult, especially in an industry where many people are still trying to find their footing. However, with a strategic approach, you can identify individuals who may be able to provide valuable guidance.

Networking at Crypto Conferences and Events: Conferences, such as Consensus or Blockchain Expo, are great places to meet experienced traders, developers, and investors who may be open to mentoring. These events often feature panel discussions, workshops, and networking sessions where you can establish connections with potential mentors.

Engaging with Thought Leaders on Social Media Platforms: As mentioned, many successful crypto traders and influencers share insights and offer guidance through platforms like X, LinkedIn, and YouTube. By engaging with these thought leaders, asking insightful questions, and demonstrating a genuine interest in learning, you can begin to build a relationship that may lead to mentorship.

Local Cryptocurrency Enthusiast Groups: Platforms like Meetup.com are designed to help like minded enthusiasts connect and hold in-person meetings.

How to Build a Successful Mentor-Mentee Relationship

Setting Clear Goals and Expectations: From the outset, it's important to communicate your goals to your mentor. Whether you're aiming to become proficient in **technical analysis**, learn about **altcoin trading**, or improve your **risk management**, setting clear expectations helps your mentor tailor their advice.

Regular Communication and Progress Updates: A mentor-mentee relationship thrives on regular communication. Ensure you **check-in** periodically, updating your mentor on your progress, challenges, and new insights. These progress updates allow your mentor to provide targeted advice that will help you improve.

Examples of Successful Mentorships

Case Study of a Mentee's Growth Under a Mentor's Guidance: One successful case involves a novice crypto trader who was struggling with understanding chart patterns and market cycles. After seeking out a mentor who was a professional in technical analysis, the mentee was able to develop a systematic approach to trading, improving both their understanding of the market and their profitability over time.

Examples of Mentorship Programs Offered by Crypto Companies: Some companies in the crypto space have formal mentorship programs designed to help new traders succeed. For example, platforms like Crypto.com and

Binance offer training programs and mentorship for individuals looking to dive deeper into crypto trading and blockchain development.

Building Your Personal Crypto Network

Your **personal crypto network** is a valuable asset that can open doors to new opportunities and insights. One benefit of having a personal crypto network, which we've already explored, is having access to exclusive insights and information. Having a strong network of crypto professionals allows you to gain access to exclusive information and early-stage developments that are not widely publicized, and your network can provide you with opportunities to collaborate on new crypto projects, whether it's developing a new coin or creating a decentralized application.

However, networking also often leads to **job opportunities**, whether it's in **blockchain development**, **crypto trading**, or other areas of the industry. Networking can further open the door to **collaborations** on exciting new projects, from launching **new tokens** to creating **decentralized finance (DeFi)** applications.

4.5 The Journey Ahead: Becoming a Savvy Crypto Trader

Becoming a **successful crypto trader** is a journey that takes time, resilience, and continuous learning. There is no shortcut to success, but with the right resources, guidance, and strategies, anyone can master the art of trading cryptocurrencies.

Characteristics of a Savvy Crypto Trader

Adaptability to Changing Market Conditions: Crypto traders must be able to adapt to the market's volatility, moving quickly in response to changing conditions.

Continuous Learning and Self-Improvement: Crypto markets evolve constantly, and traders must be committed to continuous learning to stay competitive.

The Path to Becoming a Proficient Trader

Mastering Technical and Fundamental Analysis: A deep understanding of both technical analysis and fundamental analysis is key to successful crypto trading.

Developing a Personalized Trading Strategy: Every trader must create a strategy that aligns with their own goals, risk tolerance, and knowledge.

Tips for Sustaining Long-Term Success in Crypto Trading

Balancing Trading with Personal Life: It's important to strike a balance between trading and personal time to avoid burnout.

Keeping Emotions in Check and Staying Disciplined: Emotions can cloud judgment, especially during volatile periods. Successful traders stay disciplined and stick to their strategies. Having a support network goes a long way in helping with this.

The Importance of Perseverance and Resilience

Embracing Failures as Learning Opportunities: Even experienced traders face setbacks. Every loss should be viewed as an opportunity to learn and improve.

Celebrating Small Victories and Achievements: Recognizing small wins along the way can help keep you motivated and focused on your long-term goals.

* * *

In this chapter, we've explored the emotional side of trading—how to understand and manage fear and greed, develop a disciplined mindset, maintain emotional stability in volatile markets, and build confidence through continuous learning and practice. Mastering these psychological elements will help achieve success in the ever-changing world of trading.

In conclusion, the cryptocurrency ecosystem is shaped by a variety of key players, platforms, and trends. Understanding the roles of developers, investors, regulatory bodies, and media outlets is essential for navigating this rapidly evolving industry. Whether you are a seasoned investor or just starting, staying informed about the latest developments and understanding how these entities influence the space will help you make smarter decisions in the world of cryptocurrency.

The journey to becoming a proficient and successful crypto trader is not one that should be undertaken alone. Building a **supportive network**, engaging with **communities**, and seeking out **mentorship** can significantly enhance your understanding of the crypto market and offer the emotional support needed during its volatile swings. Whether it's learning from shared experiences, collaborating on innovative projects, or gaining advice from industry experts, being an active participant in the crypto ecosystem empowers you to make informed decisions and stay ahead of trends.

Above all, becoming a **savvy crypto trader** requires more than just technical know-how; it demands resilience, discipline, and the ability to adapt to an unpredictable market. By embracing the power of community, mentorship, and continuous education, you set yourself up for sustained success and growth in the exciting world of cryptocurrency trading. With determination and the right support system, you will be better equipped to navigate the complexities of this dynamic space and reach your financial and trading goals.

5

Chapter 5: Real-World Applications and Case Studies

5.1 Case Studies of Successful Crypto Investments

Cryptocurrency investment has experienced exponential growth over the last decade, with a select few individuals achieving remarkable financial success. In this section, we examine some of the most high-profile success stories of crypto investors and break down the strategies, timing, and market sentiment that helped them turn their investments into significant profits.

The Early Adoption of Bitcoin in 2011 by Individual Investors

Bitcoin, the first cryptocurrency, has seen significant price fluctuations since its inception, but those who bought it early in its lifecycle are among the most successful investors in history. In **2011**, Bitcoin was priced around **$1**, and early adopters who recognized its potential are now reaping the rewards of holding their positions through years of volatility.

One well-known example is the **Winklevoss twins**, who invested $11 million in Bitcoin in **2013** when the price was approximately $120 per Bitcoin. As the price of Bitcoin surged to over $60,000 in 2021, their investment skyrocketed to more than **$6 billion**. Their story underscores the importance of early adoption and holding a long-term perspective, which allowed them to profit from Bitcoin's monumental rise in value.

Ethereum's ICO Participants Who Held Until the 2017 Boom

Ethereum's **Initial Coin Offering (ICO)** in **2014** was another prime example of early investors benefiting from holding onto their tokens. During the ICO, the price of one **ETH token** was approximately **$0.30**. By the time Ethereum experienced a massive price boom in **2017**, ETH reached its all-time high of over **$1,400**. Early adopters who believed in Ethereum's vision—creating a decentralized platform for smart contracts and decentralized applications—were able to see incredible returns on their investments.

For example, a person who invested **$1,000** during the ICO, purchasing **3,333 ETH tokens**, would have seen their investment increase to over **$4.6 million** during the peak of the 2017 bull run. This type of early-stage investment success illustrates the potential for huge returns in the crypto market for those willing to take risks and have confidence in emerging technologies.

The Strategies Behind Successful Investments

Diversification Across Different Crypto Assets

Successful crypto investors often diversify their portfolios to reduce the impact of volatility in individual cryptocurrencies. Rather than putting all their capital into a single asset, they spread their investments across various **blockchain platforms**, **tokens**, and **projects**.

For instance, those who invested in both Bitcoin and Ethereum during their early stages enjoyed the combined benefits of two rapidly growing and complementary technologies. By diversifying, investors increased their chances of finding a winner, while simultaneously mitigating the risks associated with placing all bets on a single asset.

Holding Through Market Volatility

One key strategy for successful investors is the ability to hold through **market volatility**. The cryptocurrency market is infamous for its wild price fluctuations, with assets like Bitcoin often experiencing double-digit percentage swings within a single day. Successful investors recognize that price volatility is inherent to crypto assets and remain steadfast in their investment strategy, despite short-term fluctuations.

During the 2018 market crash, many investors panicked and sold off their holdings at a loss. However, those who held onto their positions and weathered the storm saw massive recoveries as the market surged in 2020-2021, resulting in substantial gains.Key Takeaways from Successful Investors

Importance of Patience and Long-Term Vision

Successful crypto investors often exhibit **patience** and a **long-term vision**. Instead of seeking quick profits or reacting to every market fluctuation, they stay focused on the underlying technology and the long-term potential of the cryptocurrency they're invested in. Holding onto assets for the long run, even during downturns, has proven to be a winning strategy for many early crypto adopters.

Recognizing the Potential of Emerging Technologies

Another important takeaway from successful investors is the ability to **recognize the potential of emerging technologies** early on. Ethereum, for instance, capitalized on the growing demand for decentralized applications (dApps) and smart contracts. Investors who saw the value of Ethereum's potential beyond just being a cryptocurrency profited immensely from their early involvement.

The Role of Timing and Market Sentiment

Timing is crucial in cryptocurrency investment, as market sentiment and external factors can significantly impact asset prices. Successful investors often capitalize on the dynamics of the market, timing their entry and exit points to maximize profits.

Capitalizing on Bull Markets

Bull markets, when asset prices are in a general upward trend, present a prime opportunity for crypto investors to make gains. Successful investors often identify the start of a bull market, position themselves early, and sell at or near the peak. For example, many investors capitalized on the **2017 cryptocurrency boom**, where Bitcoin and Ethereum prices surged to all-time highs.

Avoiding Panic Selling During Downturns

On the flip side, successful crypto investors avoid the common pitfall of **panic selling** during market downturns. The price of Bitcoin, Ethereum, and other cryptocurrencies can drop drastically within short timeframes, but experienced investors understand that bear markets are a normal part of the market cycle. By sticking to their strategies and resisting the urge to sell during fear-driven downturns, they can capitalize on the recovery phases that inevitably follow.

5.2 Learning from Failed Trades: What Went Wrong?

As with any financial market, the cryptocurrency space is not without its fair share of failed investments. While there are many stories of investors achieving great success, it is equally important to examine the lessons from those who experienced substantial losses. This section delves into notable failed crypto investments and analyzes the factors that contributed to their downfall.

The 2018 Crypto Market Crash and Its Aftermath

An example of failed investments was the **2018 crypto market crash**. Following the meteoric rise of Bitcoin and other cryptocurrencies in **2017**, the market experienced a massive correction in **2018**, wiping out billions of dollars in value. Many investors who bought during the peak of the market were left with substantial losses as prices plummeted.

While the crash was largely attributed to the speculative nature of the market, the failure to adhere to sound investment principles and risk management contributed to many traders' losses.

Factors Contributing to Failures

Lack of Due Diligence and Research

Many failed crypto investments can be attributed to a **lack of due diligence and research**. Some investors made impulsive decisions without fully understanding the risks, technology, or long-term potential of the projects they invested in. For example, falling for **hype** or believing in unrealistic promises of guaranteed profits can lead to major financial losses, especially in the case of speculative or fraudulent schemes like BitConnect.

Over-Leveraging and Excessive Risk-Taking

Over-leveraging, or borrowing money to increase exposure to the crypto market, was another contributing factor to investment failures. Many traders over-leveraged during the 2017 bull market, only to see their positions liquidated during the 2018 crash. Excessive risk-taking is a significant factor in the downfall of many crypto traders, as it amplifies both gains and losses, making it harder to recover from a downturn. In my case, I knew in 2018 when Bitcoin plummeted from $17,000 back down to less than

$5,000 that it was the ideal opportunity for buying Bitcoin. But with all of my savings already invested, I had no funds available to take advantage of the opportunity.

Falling for Hype and Unrealistic Promises

Falling for hype and unrealistic promises is another major reason for investment failure. The cryptocurrency market is rife with scams and speculative projects that prey on investor enthusiasm. Failing to critically evaluate projects can lead to significant losses, as seen with BitConnect and various other failed ICOs.

5.3 Real-Life Stories: Navigating the Crypto Market

In this section, we share **real-life stories** from individual investors who have navigated the crypto market, offering insights into their successes and challenges.

A Young Investor's Journey from Novice to Successful Trader

A young investor who started trading cryptocurrency in 2017 shares his journey from initial losses to achieving consistent profits. In 2017, Alex, a tech-savvy but inexperienced young investor, jumped into cryptocurrency trading during the height of the bull market. The buzz surrounding Bitcoin and altcoins captivated him, and he eagerly invested his savings without a clear strategy. Initially, Alex saw rapid gains as prices soared, but the euphoria was short-lived. When the market crashed in 2018, Alex's portfolio was wiped out by over 70%.

Feeling defeated, Alex almost gave up, but his curiosity about blockchain technology kept him engaged. Determined to succeed, he shifted his focus to education. He started reading books on financial markets, attending webinars, and following reputable crypto analysts. Instead of chasing trends, Alex learned to analyze charts, study market cycles, and assess risk.

By 2019, Alex had developed a disciplined trading strategy. He used stop-loss orders to protect his investments and diversified his portfolio to reduce risks. He also learned to manage his emotions, avoiding impulsive reactions to market swings.

Through patience and persistence, Alex turned his losses into valuable lessons. By 2021, he was consistently making profits, not by luck but through informed decisions. Alex's story highlights the importance of education, patience, and learning from mistakes as key factors in his success. By sticking to a disciplined strategy and avoiding emotional decision-making, he turned his initial failures into valuable learning experiences. This case scenario is a testament to the power of resilience, education, and disciplined trading in achieving long-term success.

A Retiree's Perspective on Using Crypto for Diversification

Susan, a recently retired school teacher, discusses how she began investing in cryptocurrency as a way to diversify her retirement portfolio. In 2019, Susan decided to explore cryptocurrency investing as a means of diversification. With decades of savings carefully managed in traditional assets like stocks and bonds, the idea of venturing into a new, fast-paced market intrigued her. She started small, purchasing Bitcoin and Ethereum, but soon found herself overwhelmed by the market's notorious volatility. The value of her investments swung wildly, and her initial enthusiasm gave way to stress and uncertainty.

Rather than retreat, Susan sought help. She joined an online crypto investment group where she connected with seasoned investors and retirees like herself. Through mentorship and community support, she began to understand the unique dynamics of the crypto market. She learned to avoid chasing trends and instead focused on long-term fundamentals. Diversification became her guiding principle: she balanced her crypto holdings with stablecoins and stuck to well-researched projects, while maintaining the majority of her portfolio in safer, traditional investments.

By 2021, Susan had developed a strategy that worked for her. She embraced dollar-cost averaging, set realistic goals, and, most importantly, built emotional resilience to ride out market fluctuations. While her crypto investments made up a small percentage of her portfolio, they added a layer of growth potential and excitement to her retirement plan.

Susan's journey highlights that it's never too late to learn. Her story underscores the importance of education and emotional resilience in navigating the crypto market. With patience, education, and the right support, even retirees can confidently navigate the crypto market and enrich their financial futures.

Challenges Faced by Crypto Enthusiasts

Navigating Regulatory Changes and Compliance

As the crypto market is still relatively young, investors face challenges related to **regulatory uncertainty**. Regulatory changes can impact the value and legitimacy of certain projects. Many investors struggle with understanding the evolving regulatory landscape, especially as different countries adopt varying stances toward cryptocurrency.

Managing Emotional Responses During Market Swings

Emotional responses to market volatility can be a significant obstacle for crypto investors. Investors often face the temptation to panic during market downturns or to buy impulsively during bull runs. Successful traders manage these emotions by adhering to a disciplined strategy and focusing on long-term goals.

Strategies Used to Overcome Challenges

Building Resilience Through Community Support and Mentorship

One of the most effective strategies for overcoming challenges is **engaging with the crypto community**. Whether through online forums, mentorship programs, or educational platforms, community support offers guidance, feedback, and motivation. Many investors have found success by sharing experiences with others and learning from the collective wisdom of the community.

Developing Personalized Strategies for Market Volatility

Successful crypto investors develop **personalized strategies** tailored to their risk tolerance and market outlook. These strategies allow them to stay focused and avoid making rash decisions based on emotion. Developing a clear plan for entry, exit, and risk management is essential for navigating the volatile crypto market.

The Impact of Community and Education

Community engagement and **continuous learning** play a pivotal role in investor success. By actively participating in **crypto forums**, attending **educational webinars**, and staying updated with market trends, investors can gain valuable insights that help them make informed decisions. Peer support and mentorship also offer encouragement and guidance during times of uncertainty.

Return to Sarah

Remember Sarah, who was contemplating investing in Bitcoin at the beginning of this book? In 2017, Sarah, a young investor fresh out of college, decided to dive into cryptocurrency trading. The allure of quick profits and the stories of Bitcoin millionaires drew her in. Armed with enthusiasm but little knowledge, she invested her savings into a few promising coins based on online hype. Within weeks, the market turned bearish, and Sarah watched her portfolio shrink by nearly 50%.

Devastated but determined, Sarah realized she needed a different approach. She began dedicating hours to learning about cryptocurrency markets, blockchain technology, and trading strategies. She joined online forums, followed experienced traders, and took courses on risk management. Slowly, her perspective shifted from chasing quick profits to building long-term skills.

By 2019, Sarah had developed a disciplined trading strategy. She focused on technical analysis, diversified her investments, and embraced hedging techniques to mitigate risks. She also kept her emotions in check, avoiding impulsive decisions driven by fear or greed.

As the years passed, Sarah's persistence paid off. She began seeing consistent profits, though modest at first. Today, Sarah looks back at her early losses not as failures but as invaluable lessons that shaped her growth. Her journey highlights the power of education, patience, and discipline in turning setbacks into success.

* * *

In conclusion, the cryptocurrency market presents significant opportunities, but it is equally fraught with challenges. By analyzing the successes and failures of past investors, we can glean valuable lessons that help shape more informed, disciplined, and effective investment strategies. Successful crypto investing requires patience, resilience, and the ability to apply lessons from both traditional finance and the unique characteristics of the crypto space. Through continuous learning, strategic planning, and community engagement, investors can better navigate the complexities of the crypto market and increase their chances of long-term success.

6

Chapter 6: Tax Implications and Legal Considerations

6.1 Navigating Tax Responsibilities for Crypto Investments

As the popularity of cryptocurrencies continues to grow, so does the scrutiny from tax authorities worldwide. Understanding how cryptocurrencies are taxed and ensuring compliance with local regulations is critical for anyone involved in the crypto space. This section will outline the tax treatment of cryptocurrencies, the taxable events that trigger tax liabilities, methods for calculating and reporting gains and losses, and tools that can help streamline the process.

The Tax Treatment of Cryptocurrencies

The classification of cryptocurrencies for tax purposes varies significantly across different jurisdictions. In most countries, cryptocurrencies are treated either as **property** or **currency**, with significant tax implications depending on the classification.

Cryptocurrency as Property: In many countries, including the United States, cryptocurrencies are treated as property for tax purposes. The Internal Revenue Service (IRS) in the U.S. considers cryptocurrency to be an asset similar to stocks or real estate, meaning that capital gains tax applies when an individual disposes of their cryptocurrency by selling it, exchanging it for another cryptocurrency, or using it to purchase goods and services.

Cryptocurrency as Currency: Some countries, however, classify cryptocurrencies as a type of **currency** or **money** for tax purposes. For example, Japan recognizes Bitcoin as a form of payment and treats it as a currency for certain tax implications, though it also has some unique tax laws for digital assets.

Capital Gains Tax: In jurisdictions where cryptocurrencies are treated as property, individuals are subject to **capital gains tax** when they sell or exchange their digital assets. Capital gains tax rates depend on how long the asset was held before sale: assets held for more than one year may be eligible for long-term capital gains rates, which are typically lower than short-term rates.

For example, in the United States, the IRS requires individuals to report capital gains on their cryptocurrency transactions by detailing the proceeds from sales or trades. The gain or loss is calculated by subtracting the **cost basis** (the amount spent to acquire the asset) from the **selling price** (the amount received upon disposal).

Taxable Events in Crypto Transactions

Several key activities involving cryptocurrencies can trigger tax liabilities. These taxable events generally arise whenever there is a change in ownership or a transaction that results in a realized gain or loss.

Buying and Selling Cryptocurrencies: The most straightforward taxable event is the **sale of cryptocurrency**. If you sell cryptocurrency for a profit, the difference between the selling price and your cost basis is considered taxable. For example, if you bought Bitcoin for $5,000 and later sold it for $10,000, the $5,000 gain is subject to capital gains tax.

Crypto-to-Crypto Trades: Trading one cryptocurrency for another is also a taxable event, even though no fiat currency is involved. If you exchange Bitcoin for Ethereum, the IRS considers this a taxable trade and expects you to report any gains or losses on the transaction. This can get complicated, as the value of cryptocurrencies fluctuates constantly, and you must calculate the cost basis for each trade.

Using Crypto for Goods and Services: Another taxable event occurs when you use cryptocurrency to pay for goods or services. In this case, the transaction is treated as a sale of the cryptocurrency, and the gain or loss is calculated based on the fair market value of the cryptocurrency at the time of the transaction. If you used Bitcoin worth $10,000 to buy a car, and you originally bought that Bitcoin for $6,000, you would have a $4,000 taxable gain.

Staking and Earning Crypto: In some cases, earning cryptocurrency through activities such as **staking** (locking up assets in a blockchain to support network security) or participating in a **fork** (where a blockchain splits into two separate chains) can also trigger taxable events. The IRS considers these earnings as **income**, and they are subject to ordinary income tax rates.

Calculating and Reporting Gains and Losses

One of the challenges in cryptocurrency taxation is calculating and reporting the **gains** and **losses** associated with each transaction. There are various accounting methods that can be employed to simplify this process.

FIFO (First In, First Out): The FIFO method assumes that the first coins you purchased are the first ones you sell or trade. This is one of the most common accounting methods used for cryptocurrency transactions, and it is often preferred by tax authorities. Under FIFO, if you bought Bitcoin at $5,000, $6,000, and $7,000, and sold 1 Bitcoin for $10,000, the gain is calculated using the **first purchase** of $5,000, resulting in a $5,000 taxable gain.

LIFO (Last In, First Out): Under the LIFO method, the most recent coins purchased are assumed to be sold first. Using the same example above, if you used LIFO, the gain would be calculated using the last purchase of $7,000, resulting in a $3,000 taxable gain. This can be beneficial in certain situations, especially when prices are fluctuating significantly.

Cost Basis and Fair Market Value: The **cost basis** of a cryptocurrency is the original amount spent to acquire it, including transaction fees. The **fair market value** is the price of the cryptocurrency at the time of the transaction (sale or exchange). Keeping detailed records of your cost basis and market value for each transaction is essential for accurate tax reporting.

Tools and Software for Tax Reporting

Several tools and platforms can help crypto investors accurately track their transactions, calculate gains and losses, and generate reports for tax filing.

CoinTracking is a popular cryptocurrency tax software that allows users to import transaction history from exchanges, calculate gains and losses, and generate detailed tax reports. It supports a wide range of cryptocurrencies and accounting methods, making it a powerful tool for both beginners and experienced traders.

CryptoTrader.Tax is another useful tool that automatically generates tax reports based on your transaction history. It integrates with many major exchanges and wallets, and it produces the necessary forms for tax filing, such as IRS Form 8949 for the U.S. Additionally, CryptoTrader.Tax helps you calculate your gains and losses using multiple accounting methods.

6.2 Understanding Legal Considerations in Crypto Trading

The legal status and regulation of cryptocurrencies are complex and vary widely across jurisdictions. The lack of clear regulations in some regions has led to uncertainty and legal challenges for crypto traders and investors. This section delves into the legal status of cryptocurrencies, the impact of securities laws on initial coin offerings (ICOs), and the importance of Know Your Customer (KYC) and Anti-Money Laundering (AML) regulations.

The Legal Status of Cryptocurrencies

The legal treatment of cryptocurrencies depends largely on the country in which they are being used. Some countries have embraced cryptocurrencies and developed clear regulatory frameworks, while others have imposed bans or severe restrictions.

Legal Tender vs. Digital Asset Classification: In some countries, cryptocurrencies are considered **legal tender**, meaning they are recognized as an official means of payment. For example, in El Salvador, Bitcoin was declared legal tender in 2021. This classification affects how cryptocurrencies are regulated and taxed. In contrast, most countries, including the United States and the European Union, classify cryptocurrencies as **digital assets** or **property** rather than currency.

Licensing Requirements for Exchanges: Most jurisdictions require cryptocurrency exchanges to be **licensed** or **registered** with relevant financial authorities. For instance, in the U.S., exchanges must comply with **Securities and Exchange Commission (SEC)** guidelines and register with the **Financial Crimes Enforcement Network (FinCEN)** to prevent money laundering. Similarly, the European Union's **5th Anti-Money Laundering Directive** mandates that exchanges implement KYC and AML measures.

The Impact of Securities Laws on ICOs and Tokens

Initial Coin Offerings (ICOs) and **token sales** are often used by crypto projects to raise capital. However, these fundraising methods can be subject to securities laws, depending on the nature of the tokens being sold.

SEC Guidelines in the U.S.: In the United States, the SEC has stated that certain **tokens** sold through ICOs may be classified as **securities**. The SEC applies the **Howey Test**, a legal test used to determine whether a transaction qualifies as an investment contract. If a token sale meets the criteria of the Howey Test, the project is required to comply with securities laws, including registration and disclosure requirements.

Howey Test for Determining Security Status: The Howey Test evaluates whether an investment is based on a common enterprise, involves the expectation of profits, and relies on the efforts of others to generate profits.

If a token sale satisfies these conditions, the token is classified as a security and must comply with securities regulations.

The Importance of KYC and AML Regulations

Know Your Customer (KYC) and Anti-Money Laundering (AML) regulations are needed for ensuring that cryptocurrency platforms do not facilitate illegal activities such as money laundering, terrorism financing, or fraud.

KYC Verification Processes: Many crypto exchanges require users to verify their identity through KYC processes before they can trade or withdraw funds. This process typically involves providing personal information such as name, address, and government-issued identification.

AML Monitoring: In addition to KYC, exchanges are also required to monitor transactions for suspicious activities that may indicate money laundering or other illegal actions. If suspicious behavior is detected, exchanges may be required to report it to the appropriate authorities.

Examples of Legal Challenges in the Crypto Industry

Ripple's Legal Battle with the SEC: Ripple, the company behind the cryptocurrency XRP, has been involved in an ongoing legal battle with the SEC over whether XRP is classified as a security. The outcome of this case could set a significant precedent for the regulation of other cryptocurrencies.

Bitfinex and Tether Investigations: Bitfinex, a major cryptocurrency exchange, and Tether, a stablecoin issuer, have faced investigations regarding the reserves backing Tether's USDT token. The case raised questions about transparency and the potential risks associated with the use of stablecoins in the crypto market.

6.3 Compliance and Reporting: What You Need to Know

Ensuring compliance with tax and regulatory obligations is critical for crypto investors and traders. Let's discuss the importance of staying compliant with regulations, reporting requirements, strategies for ensuring compliance, and resources for staying informed.

The Importance of Staying Compliant with Regulations

Adhering to tax and regulatory standards is essential to avoid legal consequences such as fines, penalties, or even criminal prosecution.

Penalties for Non-Compliance: Failure to report cryptocurrency transactions accurately or comply with regulatory requirements can lead to significant penalties. For example, in the U.S., the IRS may impose fines for failing to report cryptocurrency income or capital gains, and some individuals may face criminal charges.

Staying Updated with Regulatory Changes: Given the rapid evolution of cryptocurrency regulations, it is important to stay informed about any changes to the law. Regularly reviewing official announcements and legal advisories can help investors and traders ensure they are in compliance with current requirements.

Reporting Requirements for Crypto Holdings

In many countries, cryptocurrency holdings and transactions must be reported on tax forms.

In the U.S., cryptocurrency transactions are reported on **Form 8949**. This form requires you to detail the proceeds from each sale or exchange, the cost basis, and any resulting gains or losses.

Many jurisdictions require **annual reporting of crypto holdings**. For example, the U.K. and several other European countries require individuals to declare their crypto holdings on their annual tax returns.

Strategies for Ensuring Compliance

To ensure compliance, crypto traders should adopt best practices such as:

Regular Consultations with Tax Professionals: Given the complexity of crypto taxes, consulting with a tax professional who specializes in cryptocurrency can help ensure accurate reporting.

Keeping Detailed Records: Detailed record-keeping is essential for accurately calculating gains and losses and reporting them correctly. Tracking all transactions, including exchanges, sales, and purchases, will simplify tax reporting.

Resources for Staying Informed on Regulatory Changes

Government Websites: Tax authorities and regulatory bodies often publish guidelines and updates on their websites. For example, the IRS in the U.S. provides tax guidance for cryptocurrency transactions on its website.

Industry Newsletters and Legal Advisories: Subscribing to cryptocurrency-related newsletters, legal advisories, and blogs can help traders stay informed about the latest developments in crypto regulations.

6.4 International Perspectives on Cryptocurrency Regulations

As the crypto market operates globally, understanding international regulations is invaluable for traders who engage in cross-border transactions. Let's take a look at the global regulatory landscape, the challenges of international crypto trading, and examples of international regulatory cooperation.

The Global Regulatory Landscape for Cryptocurrencies

The approach to cryptocurrency regulation varies greatly between countries. **Crypto-Friendly Jurisdictions**: Countries such as **Switzerland** and **Malta** have developed favorable regulatory frameworks for cryptocurrency, encouraging innovation and providing clear guidelines for businesses and investors.

Restrictive Environments: Some countries, including **China** and **India,** have taken a restrictive approach to cryptocurrencies. China has imposed a **ban on crypto mining** and trading, while India has seen fluctuating stances on cryptocurrency regulations, including proposed tax proposals and discussions on a potential crypto ban.

Challenges of Cross-Border Cryptocurrency Transactions

Variations in Tax Treatment and Reporting Requirements: Cross-border crypto trading can be complicated due to varying tax treatments and reporting requirements across jurisdictions. Traders may need to comply with multiple sets of rules, which can lead to complex tax filings.

Currency Conversion and Exchange Controls: Exchange controls and currency conversion regulations can also create obstacles for international crypto transactions. Some countries impose restrictions on the conversion of cryptocurrencies into fiat currency, complicating cross-border crypto dealings.

Examples of International Regulatory Cooperation

FATF's Role in Setting International AML Standards: The **Financial Action Task Force (FATF)** is an international body that has established global **AML standards** for cryptocurrency transactions. FATF's guidelines have been adopted by many countries to combat money laundering and ensure transparency in crypto dealings.

European Union Cooperation: EU member states have been collaborating to develop a unified approach to cryptocurrency regulation, including efforts to implement the **Markets in Crypto-Assets (MiCA)** framework, which aims to create a comprehensive set of rules for crypto-asset markets.

Future Trends in Global Crypto Regulation

The regulatory landscape for cryptocurrencies is evolving rapidly, with several trends likely to shape the future:

Emerging Trends in Digital Currency Regulation: Governments are increasingly focused on regulating **stablecoins**, digital assets that are pegged to fiat currencies, as they can pose risks to financial stability. The future of digital currencies will likely involve stricter regulations surrounding these assets.

Impact of Central Bank Digital Currencies (CBDCs): Central banks around the world are exploring the issuance of **CBDCs**—digital versions of national currencies. The advent of CBDCs could significantly impact the regulatory framework for cryptocurrencies and their integration into the global financial system.

* * *

This chapter has provided a comprehensive look at the tax responsibilities, legal considerations, and compliance strategies associated with cryptocurrency investments. By understanding the tax treatment of digital assets, staying informed on legal developments, and ensuring compliance with local and international regulations, crypto investors can navigate the complex landscape of crypto trading with confidence.

7

Chapter 7: Emerging Technologies and Their Impact on Trading

7.1 The Role of Smart Contracts in Crypto Trading

In the rapidly evolving world of cryptocurrency, one of the most groundbreaking innovations is the development and implementation of **smart contracts**. These self-executing agreements have the potential to revolutionize the way business and financial transactions are conducted in the digital space. This section will define smart contracts, explore their use cases, highlight their benefits, and address the challenges associated with their implementation in crypto trading.

Smart Contracts and Their Functionality

A **smart contract** is a digital agreement that automatically executes, controls, or documents legally relevant events according to the terms encoded within it. These contracts run on blockchain networks, such as **Ethereum**, and are designed to facilitate, verify, or enforce the negotiation or performance of a contract without the need for intermediaries. Smart contracts are self-executing because they contain predefined rules that trigger specific actions once certain conditions are met.

Self-Executing Contracts with Encoded Terms: The terms of a smart contract are encoded in the form of computer code. Once the contract is deployed on a blockchain, it executes automatically when the predefined conditions are met. For example, in a simple scenario where two parties agree to exchange cryptocurrency for goods, the smart contract ensures that the goods are transferred only after the payment has been made. Once the payment is confirmed, the contract executes the transfer of goods, thereby ensuring a seamless exchange of value.

Use Cases of Smart Contracts in Trading

Smart contracts have already begun to transform various sectors, including cryptocurrency trading. Below are some of the key use cases for smart contracts in crypto trading.

Decentralized Exchanges (DEXs): Traditional centralized exchanges (CEXs), such as Coinbase and Binance, require users to trust the platform to hold their funds and execute trades. In contrast, decentralized exchanges (DEXs) use smart contracts to enable peer-to-peer transactions without the need for an intermediary. DEXs like Uniswap or SushiSwap allow users to trade cryptocurrencies directly from their wallets, with smart contracts automatically handling the execution of trades. This decentralized model reduces counterparty risk and enhances user privacy.

Automated Token Swaps and Liquidity Provision: Smart contracts play a crucial role in automated token swaps on platforms like Uniswap, where users can trade different cryptocurrencies directly without requiring a central authority. By using smart contracts to facilitate liquidity pools, users can also earn rewards for providing liquidity to decentralized platforms. These smart contracts ensure that trades are completed instantly and efficiently, without the need for manual intervention.

Tokenized Assets and Derivatives: Smart contracts have enabled the tokenization of real-world assets such as real estate or commodities. By creating tokenized versions of these assets, smart contracts allow users to trade fractional ownership, improving liquidity and accessibility. Similarly, decentralized platforms allow for the creation of crypto derivatives (such as options and futures) that are governed by smart contracts, providing a secure and transparent environment for trading.

Benefits of Using Smart Contracts

Smart contracts offer numerous advantages that can improve the efficiency, security, and accessibility of cryptocurrency trading.

Reduction of Intermediary Costs: One of the most significant benefits of using smart contracts in crypto trading is the **reduction of intermediary costs**. In traditional finance, intermediaries such as banks, brokers, or clearinghouses typically charge fees for facilitating transactions. Smart contracts eliminate the need for these intermediaries, reducing transaction costs and enabling a more cost-efficient system.

Increased Transaction Speed and Efficiency: Traditional financial transactions can take several days to settle, especially when international transfers are involved. Smart contracts, on the other hand, can execute transactions almost instantaneously once the conditions are met. This **increased speed** enhances the overall efficiency of trading processes and allows for quicker settlements, which can be especially valuable in volatile markets like cryptocurrency.

Enhanced Security and Reduced Fraud: Since smart contracts are deployed on blockchain networks, they inherit the security features of these networks, including encryption and immutability. The decentralized nature of blockchains makes it difficult for malicious actors to alter the terms of a contract or interfere with the transaction. Furthermore, the automated nature of smart contracts ensures that all actions are performed according to the pre-set rules, reducing the likelihood of fraud or human error.

Limitations and Challenges

Despite their many advantages, smart contracts come with a set of limitations and challenges that must be addressed to ensure their widespread adoption in crypto trading.

Coding Errors Leading to Vulnerabilities: Smart contracts are written in code, and like any software, they can contain bugs or errors. If a smart contract is poorly written or has a vulnerability, it could be exploited by hackers. For example, the infamous DAO hack in 2016, which resulted in a loss of $50 million in Ethereum, was caused by a vulnerability in a smart contract. Even though the Ethereum network was able to implement a hard fork to reverse the damage, this event highlighted the risks associated with poorly written code.

Legal Implications and Enforceability: While smart contracts are self-executing, their legal enforceability is still a gray area. In many jurisdictions, the legal system has not fully integrated smart contracts into traditional contract law. While a smart contract may automatically execute its terms, it may not hold up in court if one of the parties disputes the agreement. Furthermore, the lack of legal recourse in case of a dispute could make some individuals hesitant to use smart contracts for larger transactions.

7.2 DeFi: Decentralized Finance and Its Opportunities

Decentralized Finance (DeFi) is one of the most transformative movements in the cryptocurrency space, providing an alternative to traditional financial services without relying on intermediaries like banks. This section will explore the concept of DeFi, its applications, benefits, risks, and its potential impact on traditional financial systems.

The Concept of Decentralized Finance (DeFi)

DeFi refers to the ecosystem of decentralized applications (dApps) and protocols that aim to recreate and improve upon traditional financial services using blockchain technology. The primary goal of DeFi is to provide open, permissionless financial services that anyone with an internet connection can access, regardless of geographic location or financial status. DeFi platforms operate on decentralized blockchains like Ethereum and leverage smart contracts to automate processes.

Financial Services Without Traditional Intermediaries: While traditional financial systems often rely on intermediaries, such as banks, brokers, and payment processors, to facilitate transactions, these intermediaries can introduce delays, additional fees, and access barriers. DeFi eliminates intermediaries by using smart contracts to facilitate transactions directly between parties, creating a more efficient, transparent, and inclusive financial system.

Blockchain-Based Infrastructure for DeFi: DeFi platforms are typically built on public blockchains, such as Ethereum, which provides the infrastructure for smart contracts to execute and interact with users. These decentralized platforms enable users to access various financial services, including **lending**, **borrowing**, **trading**, and **staking**.

Key DeFi Applications and Protocols

DeFi has already given rise to several innovative platforms that offer financial services and tools traditionally provided by banks and financial institutions.

Lending and Borrowing Platforms (e.g., Aave): DeFi lending platforms like Aave allow users to lend their cryptocurrencies to others in exchange for interest, or borrow assets using their crypto holdings as collateral. These platforms operate without intermediaries and use smart contracts to facilitate transactions, ensuring that lending and borrowing are done transparently and securely.

Yield Farming and Staking Opportunities: Yield farming involves providing liquidity to DeFi platforms in exchange for rewards, typically in the form of additional tokens. Similarly, staking allows users to lock up their cryptocurrencies in a protocol to earn interest or participate in network consensus. DeFi platforms have introduced new ways to generate returns on crypto holdings, offering opportunities for higher yields compared to traditional financial products.

Benefits and Risks of DeFi

DeFi presents numerous opportunities but also carries substantial risks.

Access to Financial Services for the Unbanked: One of the most significant benefits of DeFi is its potential to provide financial services to unbanked populations. By eliminating traditional intermediaries and enabling peer-to-peer transactions, DeFi platforms offer access to banking services for individuals who may not have access to traditional banks or financial institutions.

Smart Contract Risks and Platform Instability: Despite its potential, DeFi comes with significant risks, particularly related to smart contract vulnerabilities and platform instability. Hacks, bugs, and exploits in DeFi protocols can lead to loss of funds. Additionally, the decentralized nature of DeFi means that there is often no central authority to turn to in case of disputes, which can complicate risk management.

The Impact of DeFi on Traditional Finance

DeFi is not only reshaping the cryptocurrency landscape but also challenging traditional financial institutions.

Potential for Disrupting Banking Services: DeFi platforms have the potential to disrupt traditional banking services by offering alternatives for lending, borrowing, and trading. By removing intermediaries, DeFi can lower fees and provide faster, more accessible financial services.

Collaboration Between DeFi Projects and Traditional Financial Institutions: While DeFi poses a threat to traditional financial systems, many banks and financial institutions are beginning to explore partnerships and collaborations with DeFi projects. For instance, some banks are using blockchain technology for faster international payments, while others are exploring tokenized assets and stablecoins as ways to improve the efficiency of their services.

7.3 How AI and Machine Learning Are Changing Crypto Trading

The integration of Artificial Intelligence (AI) and Machine Learning (ML) into cryptocurrency trading represents a significant leap forward in optimizing trading strategies, enhancing market analysis, and automating decision-making processes. This section explores the role of AI and ML in crypto trading, their applications, benefits, challenges, and ethical considerations.

The Role of AI and Machine Learning in Trading

AI and ML are revolutionizing the world of cryptocurrency trading by providing tools that analyze large datasets, predict market trends, and automate trading decisions.

Predictive Analytics for Market Forecasting: AI and ML models can be trained to analyze historical price data, trading volumes, and other relevant market indicators to predict future price movements. These models can help traders identify potential market trends, improving the accuracy of their predictions and enabling more informed decision-making.

Algorithmic Trading and Automation: Algorithmic trading involves using AI-driven algorithms to automatically execute trades based on predefined criteria, such as price movements, order book data, or news sentiment. These algorithms can execute trades much faster than humans, making them particularly useful in volatile markets like cryptocurrency.

Machine Learning Models for Market Analysis

Machine learning models, particularly those based on neural networks, are increasingly being used to analyze and predict market trends in cryptocurrency trading.

Neural Networks for Price Prediction: Neural networks, a subset of machine learning, are widely used for price prediction in crypto markets. These networks are trained on historical data to recognize patterns and predict future price movements, offering traders valuable insights into market trends.

Sentiment Analysis of Social Media Data: Another application of AI in crypto trading is sentiment analysis. By analyzing social media platforms like X, Reddit, and news outlets, AI tools can gauge the market's sentiment and make predictions based on public opinions and discussions about specific cryptocurrencies. This can help traders capitalize on trends before they become widely known.

Advantages of AI-Driven Trading

The integration of AI into cryptocurrency trading offers several advantages:

Enhanced Decision-Making Through Data Analysis: AI-driven trading systems can analyze vast amounts of data in real-time, enabling traders to make more accurate and timely decisions. This improves the overall decision-making process and allows traders to react quickly to market changes.

Reduced Emotional Bias in Trading: Human traders are often subject to emotional biases, such as fear and greed, which can lead to irrational decision-making. AI systems, however, make decisions based purely on data and predefined criteria, eliminating emotional biases from trading strategies.

Challenges and Ethical Considerations

While AI-driven trading offers numerous advantages, it also poses challenges and ethical dilemmas:

Data Privacy and Security Concerns: AI systems rely heavily on large datasets, which can include sensitive information about traders and market activity. Ensuring the privacy and security of this data is critical to prevent breaches and misuse.

Over-Reliance on Machines and the Risk of Systemic Errors: One potential drawback of AI in crypto trading is the risk of over-reliance on machines. If traders and investors rely too heavily on automated systems without fully understanding their underlying mechanisms, they may expose themselves to significant risks, especially if a machine learning model malfunctions or makes incorrect predictions.

7.4 The Future of Crypto: Trends to Watch

The cryptocurrency landscape is constantly evolving, with several emerging trends that are poised to shape the future of the industry. In this section, we will highlight some of these trends, including the rise of **non-fungible tokens (NFTs)**, the impact of **central bank digital currencies (CBDCs)**, and the role of **regulation** and technological innovations in the future of crypto.

Emerging Trends in Cryptocurrency

Several trends are likely to influence the future development of cryptocurrency:

Growth of Non-Fungible Tokens (NFTs): NFTs have gained significant attention in recent years, with digital art, collectibles, and virtual assets being sold for millions of dollars. These tokens, which represent unique digital assets, are expected to continue growing in popularity, particularly in industries like gaming, art, and entertainment.

Integration of Blockchain with IoT Devices: The integration of blockchain technology with Internet of Things (IoT) devices is another trend to watch. Internet of Things is the network of physical objects embedded with software and smart devices. Examples include smart appliances, smart watches, smart thermostats, smart televisions, and self-driving cars. Blockchain can provide secure, decentralized data management for IoT devices, offering solutions to challenges such as **data integrity**, **security**, and **interoperability**.

The Potential Impact of Central Bank Digital Currencies (CBDCs)

CBDCs are digital versions of national currencies issued and regulated by central banks. These digital currencies have the potential to revolutionize the cryptocurrency landscape by offering more secure, stable alternatives to existing cryptocurrencies.

CBDCs could compete with existing cryptocurrencies like Bitcoin and Ethereum by offering greater stability, as they would be pegged to fiat currencies. However, this could also make cryptocurrencies less attractive for speculation.

CBDCs could also facilitate faster, cheaper cross-border transactions, potentially integrating with blockchain-based systems to enhance global financial systems.

The Role of Regulation in Crypto's Future

As cryptocurrencies continue to grow in popularity, regulatory frameworks are expected to evolve. Governments worldwide are starting to take a more active role in regulating the cryptocurrency industry. Increased **scrutiny** and **compliance requirements** will likely shape the future of crypto, with tighter rules on anti-money laundering (AML) and know-your-customer (KYC)protocols.

Innovation in Regulatory Technology (RegTech): The rise of RegTech—the use of technology to comply with regulations—will likely play a significant role in the future of crypto. Innovative technologies like smart contracts and blockchain could streamline compliance processes, ensuring that crypto projects can meet regulatory requirements while maintaining decentralized principles.

The Technological Advancements Driving Crypto

Several technological innovations are driving the future of cryptocurrency:

Quantum Computing and Its Implications for Cryptography: Quantum computing has the potential to disrupt current cryptographic systems. As quantum computers become more powerful, there will be a need to develop new cryptographic algorithms that are resistant to quantum attacks, ensuring the security of blockchain networks.

Advancements in Blockchain Scalability Solutions: Blockchain scalability remains a critical challenge for cryptocurrency networks. However, innovations like **layer-2 solutions** (e.g., **Lightning Network**) and **sharding** are expected to improve transaction speeds and scalability, paving the way for more widespread adoption of cryptocurrencies. The Lightning Network is an off-chain network of payment channels that reduces transaction speed and cost. Sharding is a method of dividing the blockchain into smaller, more efficient units.

* * *

This chapter has examined several critical aspects of the evolving cryptocurrency landscape, including **smart contracts**, **DeFi**, **AI and machine learning** in trading, and the emerging trends that are likely to shape the future of the industry. As technology and regulation continue to evolve, the future of cryptocurrency holds immense potential for innovation, disruption, and growth.

8

Conclusion

Throughout this book, we have journeyed through the fundamental concepts that shape the world of cryptocurrency and blockchain technology. We began by exploring the basics of blockchain, understanding its decentralized nature, and how cryptocurrencies, like Bitcoin and Ethereum, utilize this technology to revolutionize traditional financial systems. From there, we moved into practical strategies for investing in cryptocurrencies, emphasizing the importance of diversification and long-term vision.

The book delved into the critical aspects of risk management, technical and fundamental analysis, and the growing need for robust security measures to protect your digital assets. We also touched on the regulatory environment and tax responsibilities surrounding cryptocurrency investments, ensuring that you are prepared for the legal and financial implications of your trades.

Emerging technologies such as smart contracts, DeFi, and AI-driven trading were explored to give you a sense of the future of crypto and how you can leverage these innovations for success. We also examined the psychological aspects of trading, discussing the importance of emotional discipline, mental resilience, and strategies to overcome fear and greed. Real-life examples and case studies provided insights into the practical applications of these concepts, while the value of community, mentorship, and continuous learning was emphasized as crucial elements in any trader's journey.

The key lessons throughout this book highlight the need for a solid understanding of blockchain basics as the foundation of successful cryptocurrency trading. We've learned that diversification in your portfolio is paramount, reducing risk and providing a better opportunity for consistent growth. Risk management and the ability to detect scams are essential skills in navigating the volatility of crypto markets. Equally important are robust security protocols that protect your assets from theft and hacking.

Moreover, continuous learning and staying updated on emerging technologies, trends, and regulatory changes are necessary for long-term success. The importance of community engagement and mentorship cannot be overstated—these networks of knowledge and support will empower you to make better decisions and foster growth, both professionally and personally, in your trading endeavors.

As you move forward with your cryptocurrency trading, remember to apply the knowledge and strategies shared in this book. Start small, invest time in thorough research, and don't be afraid to test your strategies with a diversified portfolio. Keep refining your approach based on the insights you've gained and adapt to changing market conditions. Remember, the crypto market is dynamic, and successful traders are those who can learn, adapt, and evolve with it.

In a space as rapidly evolving as cryptocurrency, the ability to stay informed is key. Trends shift, new technologies emerge, and regulations evolve. By committing to continuous learning, whether through news updates, workshops, or forums, you ensure that you remain competitive and relevant in the ever-changing crypto landscape. Make it a habit to stay curious, invest in your education, and embrace the learning process as an ongoing journey.

Now, equipped with the tools, strategies, and insights from this book, you are ready to take on the cryptocurrency market with confidence and preparedness. Whether you are just starting out or have been trading for some time, the key is to take action and trust in your ability to learn and grow. Use this book as a foundational guide to navigate the complexities of the market, knowing that with the right mindset and approach, you can achieve your financial goals.

I encourage you to engage with crypto communities, seek out mentorship, and participate in discussions and forums where you can continue to enhance your understanding and refine your trading skills. The value of connecting with like-minded individuals and gaining insights from experienced traders cannot be underestimated. Be an active participant in the crypto space, sharing knowledge and learning from others, as this will be one of the most rewarding aspects of your journey.

Crypto trading is not just about numbers; it's also about personal growth. You will face challenges, market volatility, and emotional highs and lows. However, by maintaining emotional discipline, practicing mental resilience, and celebrating your achievements along the way, you will develop the fortitude to navigate both the ups and downs of the market. Remember, success in crypto trading is as much about personal development as it is about financial success.

The world of cryptocurrency offers vast opportunities, and with the right tools, knowledge, and mindset, you are well-positioned to thrive in this exciting and dynamic space. Embrace the journey with confidence and an open mind, knowing that your potential for success is unlimited. With persistence, resilience, and a commitment to continuous learning, the crypto market can become a powerful vehicle for achieving your financial goals. Stay curious, stay determined, and most importantly—keep growing as you shape your future as a savvy and successful crypto trader.

* * *

Keeping the Game Alive

Now that you've explored the essentials of cryptocurrency trading and gained the tools to create your own winning strategy, it's time to share what you've learned and help others discover the same path to success.

By leaving an honest review of this book on Amazon, you're doing more than sharing your thoughts—you're guiding other beginner traders toward the resource they need to kick-start their journey. Your words could be the spark that fuels someone else's passion for cryptocurrency trading.

Thank you for being part of this journey. The world of trading grows stronger and more vibrant when we pass on our knowledge, and with your help, we're keeping that momentum alive.

Scan the QR code below to leave your review on Amazon.

Let's keep empowering others—together!

Sincerely,
Linda Beach

References

Books:

1. Nakamoto, S. (2008). *Bitcoin: A Peer-to-Peer Electronic Cash System.* Bitcoin.org.
2. Tapscott, D., & Tapscott, A. (2016). *Blockchain Revolution: How the Technology Behind Bitcoin Is Changing Money, Business, and the World.* Penguin.
3. Antonopoulos, A. M. (2017). *Mastering Bitcoin: Unlocking Digital Cryptocurrencies.* O'Reilly Media.
4. Buterin, V. (2014). *A Next-Generation Smart Contract and Decentralized Application Platform.* Ethereum Whitepaper.

Academic Articles:

1. Catalini, C., & Gans, J. S. (2016). Some Simple Economics of the Blockchain. *MIT Sloan Research Paper* No. 5191-16.
2. Yermack, D. (2017). Corporate Governance and Blockchains. *Review of Finance,* 21(1), 7-31.
3. Zohar, A. (2015). Bitcoin and Beyond: The Possibilities and Limits of Decentralized Consensus. *IEEE Internet Computing,* 19(6), 18-28.

Websites:

1. CoinMarketCap. (2025). *Cryptocurrency Prices and Market Data.* https://www.coinmarketcap.com
2. CoinTelegraph. (2025). *Blockchain and Cryptocurrency News.* https://w

ww.cointelegraph.com

3. Glassnode. (2025). *On-chain Market Intelligence*. https://www.glassnode.com
4. CryptoCompare. (2025). *Cryptocurrency Market Data and Analysis*. https://www.cryptocompare.com

Reports and Whitepapers:

1. Bitcoin.org. (2009). *Bitcoin Whitepaper*. https://bitcoin.org/bitcoin.pdf
2. Ethereum Foundation. (2015). *Ethereum Whitepaper*. https://github.com/ethereum/wiki/wiki/White-Paper

Online Forums:

1. BitcoinTalk. (2025). *Bitcoin Forum – The World's Largest Cryptocurrency Community*. https://bitcointalk.org
2. Reddit. (2025). *r/CryptoCurrency – Cryptocurrency News, Discussion, and Analysis*. https://www.reddit.com/r/CryptoCurrency/

Blogs and News Outlets:

1. Kharif, O. (2018). "Bitcoin Has a New Rival: It's Called Ethereum." *Bloomberg*. https://www.bloomberg.com
2. Buterin, V. (2023). "The Future of Ethereum." *Ethereum Blog*. https://blog.ethereum.org

Courses and Online Learning:

1. Coursera. (2025). *Bitcoin and Cryptocurrency Technologies*. https://www.coursera.org/learn/cryptocurrency
2. Udemy. (2025). *Blockchain and Cryptocurrency Explained*. https://www.udemy.com/course/blockchain-and-cryptocurrency-explained

Government and Legal Sources:

1. U.S. Securities and Exchange Commission (SEC). (2020). *Investor Bulletin: Initial Coin Offerings (ICO).* https://www.sec.gov
2. European Central Bank (ECB). (2019). *The Economics of Cryptocurrencies: Bitcoin and Beyond.* https://www.ecb.europa.eu

Podcasts and Webinars:

1. *Unchained* (2025). "The Crypto Frontier." https://www.unchainedpodcast.com
2. *The Pomp Podcast* (2025). "Bitcoin and Crypto with Anthony Pompliano." https://www.anthonypompliano.com/podcast

Social Media Influencers:

1. Saylor, M. (2025). *Michael Saylor's Twitter Profile.* https://www.twitter.com/michael_saylor
2. Vitalik Buterin. (2025). *Vitalik Buterin's Twitter Profile.* https://www.twitter.com/vitalikbuterin

www.ingramcontent.com/pod-product-compliance
Lightning Source LLC
LaVergne TN
LVHW022050200926
848481LV00003B/856
9798295470639